Study Guide
To Accompany

Computers & Information Systems
Tools for an Information Age

Third Edition

H.L. Capron

The Benjamin/Cummings Publishing Company, Inc.

Redwood City, California ■ Menlo Park, California
Reading, Massachusetts ■ New York ■ Don Mills, Ontario
Wokingham, U.K. ■ Amsterdam ■ Bonn ■ Sydney
Singapore ■ Tokyo ■ Madrid ■ San Juan

Printed in the United States of America. Published simultaneously in Canada.

ISBN 0-8053-1291-9

1 2 3 4 5 6 7 8 9 10--AL--96 95 94 93 92

The Benjamin/Cummings Publishing Company, Inc.
390 Bridge Parkway
Redwood City, California 94065

To the Student

The purpose of this study guide is to reinforce the concepts presented in the text, both to increase your computer literacy and to help you improve your test scores.

Study materials presented are as follows:

Learning Objectives

These will let you know what concepts and facts you should understand by the time you have read the chapter.

Why This Chapter Is Important

This section shows you how the chapter relates to you, or to the computer industry, society, to other chapters in the text, or to advanced courses you may take in the future.

Chapter Outline

This chapter overview provides a quick preview of what is in the chapter, and can serve as a review/recall tool after you have read the chapter.

Key Words

You should become familiar with each of the terms listed here. If you are unsure of any of them, check them in the glossary in the text. Also, this list will be helpful when answering test questions in the chapter.

Study Hints

Some clues on what to remember and how to remember it.

Self-Test

Test yourself on the material in this chapter. Most chapters contain multiple choice, true/false, matching, and fill-in questions that reflect the contents of the chapter. By taking these tests, you will have a head start in doing well on class examinations.

Test Answers

The answers let you know *now* how you are doing. Immediate feedback.

Close to Home

This feature relates the text material to you and your daily life, and shows how the computer is a part of all our lives.

Extra Notes

Few of the extra offerings are intended to be serious additions to your study. Most are intended only to lighten up the study hours a bit.

I wish you well as you begin your study of computers, since you will, in some way, always have a relationship with them.

H. L. Capron

Contents

The Age of Information: Reaching for New Tools

Learning Objectives

- ❑ Appreciating the breadth and drama of the Information Age.
- ❑ Understanding computer anxiety and appreciating why our society can no longer do without computers.
- ❑ Understanding the meaning of and need for computer literacy.
- ❑ Understanding the extent of the computer's impact on government, paperwork, robotics, money, transportation, commerce, energy, health and medicine, agriculture, graphics, education, the sciences, training, the home, and human beings.

Why This Chapter Is Important

This chapter contains very little technical information, but it is an excellent springboard for the technical information to follow. Once you truly understand the pervasiveness of the computer in our society and the services it provides, you must agree with the conclusion that our society could no longer function effectively without computers. The final conclusion is our need for computer literacy; hence the motivation to pursue the technical information in the subsequent chapters of the book.

JUST ORDER BOSSY A PIZZA

Cows may soon be munching on pizza and all sorts of other hitherto forbidden goodies. In fact, using computer analysis, researchers have found that when these items are mixed in with the regular feed, the result is nutritious.

The idea is to save money on feed and also save disposal costs by feeding cows foods that have outlived their human-consumption shelf lives. Current efforts have yielded a tasty combination of left over chocolate eggs, pizza, and canned vegetables.

Chapter Outline

- Stepping Out
  - Forging a Computer-Based Society
  - A Computer in Your Future
- Worry about Computers? Me?
- Computer Literacy for All
  - The Haves and the Have-Nots
  - So Here You Are in a Computer Class
- Everywhere You Turn
  - The Nature of Computers
  - Where Computers Are Used
- Toward Computer Literacy

THEY USED TO BE MOVIES

Here are some movies whose themes were used as the basis for computer video games: Raiders of the Lost Ark, The China Syndrome, Superman, King Kong, Jaws, and the Empire Strikes Back.

Close to Home

Did some of the phrases in the chapter strike a familiar note? When it comes to computer anxiety, many people are relieved to find that they are not the only ones who are uncomfortable with the idea of computers. Perhaps, on the other hand, you feel very comfortable with computers but recognize a need for more knowledge. No matter what category you may fall in, you will be well served by taking this course. New worlds are about to unfold for you.

MONOPOLY

Computer analysis by Irvin Hetzel of Iowa State University has revealed the 10 squares most likely to be hit during a game of Monopoly. In order, they are: Illinois Avenue, Go, B&O Railroad, Free Parking, Tennessee Avenue, New York Avenue, Reading Railroad, St. James Place, Water Works, and Pennsylvania Railroad.

CHAPTER

1

Overview of a Computer System: Hardware, Software, and People

Learning Objectives

- ❑ Introduction to personal computers.
- ❑ Familiarization with the basic components of a computer system: input, processing, output, and storage.
- ❑ Acquaintance with some common input, output, and storage media.
- ❑ Introduction to the various sizes of computers and to centralized versus decentralized computer systems.
- ❑ Introduction to software, including common applications software.
- ❑ Introduction to people who use and run a computer system.

Why This Chapter Is Important

From a technical standpoint, this chapter is really the first chapter of the book. For many of you, it may be the first time you have had any understanding of what the rest of the world (or so it seems) is talking about.

Take it a little bit slow. There is an enormous amount of information in this chapter and much of it may be entirely new to you. This is a chapter you may want to read carefully more than once, so you can give yourself a solid foundation on which to build.

Remember that most of the information in this chapter will be explained in much greater detail in subsequent chapters. You may, in fact, want to review this chapter again later, to help you put some of the later chapters in perspective.

Chapter Outline

The Beginning of What You Need to Know

Hardware: Meeting the Machine
- Your Personal Computer Hardware
- Input: What Goes In
- The Processor and Memory: Data Manipulation
- Output: What Comes Out
- Secondary Storage
- The Complete Hardware System
- Traditional Classification of Computers
  - Mainframes and Supercomputers
  - Minicomputers
  - Personal Computers
- Data Communications: Processing Here or There

Software: Telling the Machine What to Do
- Software for Your Personal Computer
- The Big Five: Application Software
  - Word processing/Desktop publishing
  - Electronic Spreadsheets
  - Database Management
  - Graphics
  - Data Communications
- What Programmers Do

People and Computers
- Computers and You, the User
- Computer People
- The End-User Revolution

The End of the Beginning

COMPUTER WIMP

You would think that a fellow with a Ph.D. would not be frightened of computers. However, John Bear, Ph.D., became so distressed about using his personal computer that he wrote a book to express his rage and frustration. He called his book *Computer Wimp*. But that was a dozen years ago. Now, flush with computer sophistication, Mr. Bear is at it again; his new book is called *Computer Wimp No More*. Having achieved "computer happiness," he has written his most recent book to spare others his fate.

Mr. Bear begins by distinguishing hardware from software, and then glides forward through standard topics, inserting pep talks along the way. In his breezy style he also tackles more esoteric subjects, such as buying by mail, overcoming technobabble, and the psychological problems associated with computers. For those still in paralysis, he devotes a chapter called "Maybe I Could Just Die Early" - and, presumably, skip computers altogether.

MUMBO JUMBO: IT COULD BE WORSE

Overwhelmed with technical jargon? Try some of these: FTAM, T-1, MRO, R2, IDE, PCL, SCSI, ISV, and PCMCIA. Columnist John Dvorak asked a dozen computer luminaries the meaning of "client-server computing" and received a dozen different answers. Don't expect much change in the future.

Key Words

Application software ________________

Bar code ________________

Bar code reader ________________

Centralization ________________

Central processing unit (CPU) ________________

Chief information officer (CIO) ________________

Communications software ________________

Computer ________________

Computer Information Systems (CIS) ________________

Computer operator ________________

Computer programmer ________________

Computing Services ________________

Console ________________

Data ________________

Data communications ________________

Data entry operator ________________

Database management ________________

Decentralization ________________

Digital audio tape (DAT) ________________

Disk drive ________________

Disk pack

Diskette

Distributed data processing (DDP)

Documentation

Electronic spreadsheet

End-user revolution

Floppy disk

Graphics

Hard disk

Hardware

Information

Information services

Input

Input device

Keyboard

Librarian

Local area network (LAN)

Magnetic disk

Magnetic tape

Mainframe

Management Information Services

Memory

Microcomputer ______________________

Micro-to-mainframe link ______________________

Minicomputer ______________________

Mouse ______________________

Network ______________________

Optical disk ______________________

Output ______________________

Packaged software ______________________

Pen-based computer ______________________

Peripheral equipment ______________________

Primary storage ______________________

Printer ______________________

Processor ______________________

Program ______________________

Scanner ______________________

Screen ______________________

Secondary storage ______________________

Software ______________________

Speech recognition ______________________

Supercomputer ______________________

Supermicro ______________________

Supermini ______________________

INTRODUCING NEW PRODUCTS

If you came up with a new product, would you rent an airplane to tell the world about it? Perhaps you would buy advertising on TV or pass out free samples door-to-door. All these approaches are costly. Furthermore, it would be unfortunate if you spent a lot of money only to discover that the public was not interested in your product.

Large enterprises such as Proctor & Gamble Co. have historically invested years and millions of dollars to introduce their products to some segment of the population. The very slowness of the process opened the door for copy-cat competitors to rush in with their version of the new product.

Since reducing costs and increasing speed are two goals of market testing, a rescue operation using computers was a natural. Modern researchers give product samples to a select group of consumers, then quickly follow up for their reactions. This data is input to a computer, which factors it into historical data patterns and produces sales projections. The whole process takes just three or four months and costs about a fourth of the expense using the old methods.

Systems analyst ____________________

Tape drive ____________________

Terminal ____________________

User friendly ____________________

Voice input ____________________

Wand reader ____________________

Word processing ____________________

Workstation ____________________

Study Hints

This chapter requires a lot of memorization. It may seem as if you need to know everything about computer systems right from the beginning of the text.

A couple of things could help you get the hardware points firmly entrenched - a tour of a local computer installation and/or a tour of your own local small computer store. Your instructor may have a class tour in mind; if not, consider arranging one yourself. Many business installations and government organizations welcome tour groups because they feel that tours promote good will in the community.

Self-Test

Multiple Choice

1. The processor is an example of
   a. software
   b. hardware
   c. a program
   d. an output unit

2. Additional data and programs not being used by the processor are stored in
   a. secondary storage
   b. output units
   c. input units
   d. the CPU

3. Step-by-step instructions that run the computer are
   a. hardware
   b. programming languages
   c. documents
   d. programs

4. A computer featuring a flat tablet:
   a. minicomputer
   b. mainframe
   c. desktop computer
   d. pen-based computer

5. Desktop and personal computers are other names for
   a. microcomputers
   b. mainframes
   c. minicomputers
   d. peripheral equipment

6. The raw material to be processed by a computer is called
   a. a program
   b. software
   c. data
   d. information

7. Which is not a computer field job?
   a. systems analyst
   b. user
   c. data entry operator
   d. programmer

8. A wand reader is an example of a(n)
   a. processing device
   b. input device
   c. storage device
   d. output device

9. Computer people who design, write, test, and implement programs are
   a. programmers
   b. data entry people
   c. computer operators
   d. systems analysts

10. Printers and screens are common forms of
a. input units
b. storage units
c. output units
d. processing units

11. The unit that transforms data into information is the
a. CPU
b. disk drive
c. bar code reader
d. wand reader

12. People who prepare data for processing are
a. programmers
b. printers
c. librarians
d. data entry operators

13. The system whereby computers and data storage are placed in dispersed locations is known as
a. centralized processing
b. packaged software
c. summarizing
d. distributed data processing

14. An example of peripheral equipment:
a. CPU
b. printer
c. network
d. microcomputer

15. Another name for available-for-purchase software is
a. secondary software
b. packaged software
c. systems software
d. peripheral software

16. Which acronym is NOT an abbreviation for a computer department:
a. CS
b. MIS
c. CIS
d. IS

17. A device that inputs data by scanning letters and numbers is a
a. keyboard
b. bar code reader
c. wand reader
d. floppy disk

18. Another name for memory is
a. secondary storage
b. primary storage
c. disk storage
d. tape storage

19. Which is not a computer classification?
a. maxicomputer
b. microcomputer
c. minicomputer
d. mainframe

20. All processing is done in one location in a system that is
a. networked
b. centralized
c. distributed
d. linked

21. The input device that translates motions on a flat surface to the screen is the
a. wand reader
b. bar code reader
c. keyboard
d. mouse

22. Computer users who are not computer professionals are sometimes called
a. librarians
b. information officers
c. peripheral users
d. end-users

23. The most powerful computers are
a. superminis
b. supermainframes
c. supermicros
d. supercomputers

24. Raw data is processed into
a. number sheets
b. paragraphs
c. updates
d. information

25. Laser beam technology is used for
a. terminals
b. keyboards
c. optical disk
d. magnetic tape

True/False

T F 1. The processor is also called the central processing unit, or CPU.

T F 2. Secondary storage units contain the instructions and data to be used immediately by the processor.

T F 3. A computer department may be called MIS, CIS, or IS.

T F 4. Two secondary storage media are magnetic disk and magnetic tape.

T F 5. A diskette holds more data than a hard disk.

T F 6. The cost of hardware is going down.

T F 7. The most powerful microcomputers are known as supercomputers.

T F **8.** Computers are becoming accessible to more people.

T F **9.** Processed data that is organized, meaningful, and useful is called information.

T F **10.** User friendly refers to a special kind of terminal.

T F **11.** To use a computer, you need not know its internal functions.

T F **12.** The people who write software are called computer operators.

T F **13.** Word processing is a type of software.

T F **14.** Computer hardware is always kept in one large room.

T F **15.** These computers are arranged from smallest to largest: microcomputers, minicomputers, mainframes, supercomputers.

T F **16.** Magnetic tape is usually used with microcomputers.

T F **17.** A distributed data system sends data directly to each employee's personal computer.

T F **18.** A LAN is usually set up between two cities.

T F **19.** Most people in the computer field are involved with software.

T F **20.** Computer users must be highly skilled and well trained.

T F **21.** People can usually spot trends more quickly from numbers than from graphics.

T F **22.** Desktop publishing is popular in the home but not useful for business.

T F **23.** A spreadsheet is comprised of columns and rows.

T F **24.** A programmer must be able to use one or more programming languages.

T F **25.** Computers are becoming more difficult for people to use.

Matching

___	1. programs	a.	documentation
___	2. processor	b.	disk pack
___	3. instruction manual	c.	output
___	4. storage	d.	floppy disk
___	5. retain processed data	e.	software
___	6. processed data	f.	supercomputers
___	7. primary storage	g.	CPU
___	8. diskette	h.	store
___	9. printer	i.	information
___	10. most powerful computers	j.	memory

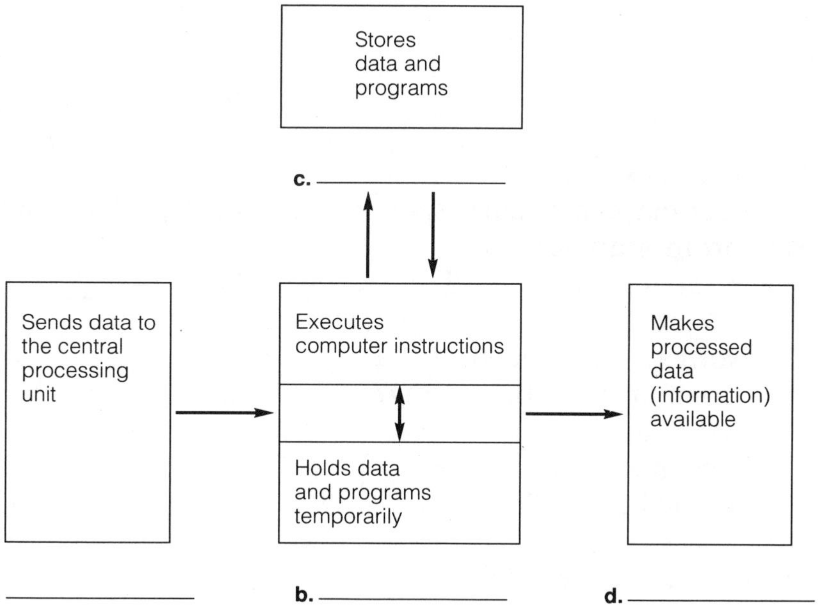

Figure 1 Four primary components of a computer system.

Fill-In

1. What are the four general hardware units of a computer?

   1.a. ____________________

   b. ____________________

   c. ____________________

   d. ____________________

2. What kind of software presents numbers in columns and rows?

   2. ____________________

3. Where is data held after it is input to the system but before it is processed?

   3. ____________________

4. What are magnetic tape reels mounted on when their data is to be read by the computer system?

   4. ____________________

5. What are the input, output, and secondary storage devices attached to a computer called?

   5. ____________________

6. What are large computers called in the computer industry?

   6. ____________________

7. What is the term describing a system whereby computers and data storage are placed in geographically separate locations?

   7. ____________________

8. What is the word for raw material that is given to a computer for processing?

   8. ____________________

9. What is the exchange of data over communication facilities called?

   9. ____________________

10. Connecting microcomputers to a mainframe is called:

    10. ____________________

11. What is software that is easy to use said to be? 11. ________________

12. What does MIS stand for? 12. ________________

13. What is the trend of users becoming knowledgeable and less dependent on computer professionals? 13. ________________

14. What are three types of input methods mentioned in the chapter? 14.a. ________________
b. ________________
c. ________________

15. What is another name for a microcomputer? 15. ________________

16. What kind of system does all its processing in one location? 16. ________________

17. List the four elements that are necessary to make a computer system work. 17.a. ________________
b. ________________
c. ________________
d. ________________

18. Who are the people who plan and design systems of programs? 18. ________________

19. What are the planned step-by-step instructions required to turn data into information? 19. ________________

20. What is BASIC an example of? 20. ________________

Test Answers

Multiple Choice

1. b	6. c	11. a	16. a	21. d
2. a	7. b	12. d	17. c	22. d
3. d	8. b	13. d	18. b	23. d
4. d	9. a	14. b	19. a	24. d
5. a	10. c	15. b	20. b	25. c

True/False

1. T	6. T	11. T	16. F	21. F
2. F	7. F	12. F	17. F	22. F
3. T	8. T	13. T	18. F	23. T
4. T	9. T	14. F	19. T	24. T
5. F	10. F	15. T	20. F	25. F

Matching

1. e	6. i
2. g	7. j
3. a	8. d
4. b	9. c
5. h	10. f

Figure

Figure 1
a. input
b. processing
c. secondary storage
d. output

Fill-In

1. a. input unit
   b. processor
   c. output unit
   d. storage unit

2. spreadsheet

3. main storage

4. tape drives

5. peripheral equipment

6. mainframes

7. distributed data processing

8. data

9. data communications

10. micro-to-mainframe link

11. user friendly

12. management information system

13. end-user revolution

14. a. keyboard
    b. bar code reader
    c. wand reader

15. personal computer

16. centralized

17. a. hardware
    b. software
    c. data
    d. people

18. systems analysts

19. software (or program)

20. programming language

Close to Home

The introductory chapter reflects the excitement associated with computers, but this chapter gives you your first real look at the cold facts, and there are many of them. How do you react to the information tumbling from the pages? This chapter should give you an appreciation of what is to come - and a determination to dig further.

CHAPTER

2

The Central Processing Unit: The Brain of the Machine

Learning Objectives

- ❑ Knowing the components of the central processing unit and how they work together.
- ❑ Understanding how the central processing unit interacts with memory.
- ❑ Understanding how program instructions are executed by the computer.
- ❑ Understanding how data is represented in the computer.
- ❑ Understanding how the computer finds instructions and data.
- ❑ Understanding primary storage components.
- ❑ Having an appreciation for computer processing speeds.

Why This Chapter Is Important

Here, in this chapter, we have the information that is central to the very existence of computers. For example, this chapter describes the important link between the physical nature of the machine operation (charge/no charge) and the mental processes of human beings (represented by the binary numbers 1/0). These two numbers, zero and one, are used as the foundation to represent, in various combinations, all the data and instructions inside the computer.

The information in this chapter will help you understand what a computer is really all about in a technical sense, beyond just knowing the kinds of things computers can do for us.

Chapter Outline

The Central Processing Unit
- The Control Unit
- The Arithmetic/Logic Unit
- Registers: Temporary Storage Areas

Memory

How the CPU Executes Program Instructions

Storage Locations and Addresses: How the Control Unit Finds Instructions and Data

Data Representation: On/Off
- Bits, Bytes, and Words
- Coding Schemes: EBCDIC and ASCII
- The Parity Bit: Checking for Errors

Inside Your Personal Computer

Microprocessor: Computer on a Chip

Memory Components
- Semiconductor Storage: Let the Chips Fall Where They May
- RAM and ROM

Computer Processing Speeds
- More Speed? What's the Rush?
- RISC Technology: Less Is More
- Parallel Processing: The Ultimate Speed Solution

Next: Future Chip Talk

WHO'S GOT THE BUTTON?

Smart buttons are here. Round and flat, they look like a watch battery, but actually contain a special chip that holds data that can be read or updated using a pen-like device attached to a portable computer. Users can attach the button with an adhesive backing to almost anything. Typical uses are stick-on buttons for hospital ID bracelets, fire extinguishers, hazardous waste drums, cargo containers, and even ID tags for livestock.

Key Words

Accumulator ______________________

Address ______________________

Address register ______________________

Arithmetic/logic unit (ALU) ______________________

Arithmetic operations ______________________

ASCII ______________________

Binary system ______________________

Biochip ______________________

Bit ______________________

Bus line ______________________

Byte ______________________

Central processing unit (CPU) ______________________

Check bit ______________________

CISC ______________________

Clock ______________________

CMOS ______________________

Control unit ______________________

Dynamic RAM (DRAM) ______________________

E-time ______________________

EBCDIC ______________________

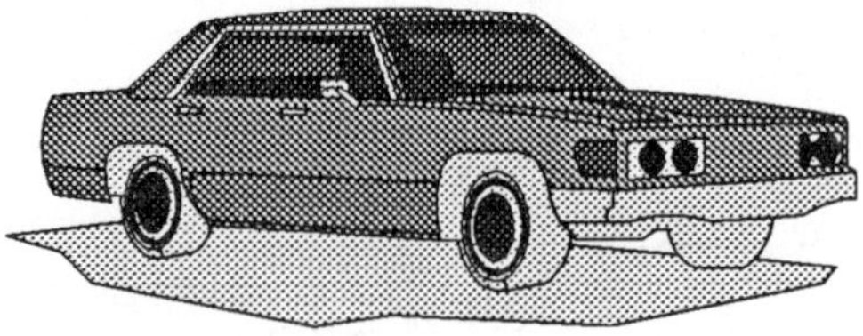

CAR CHIPS

It is not as easy to peer under the hood as it used to be. Today's mechanic is faced with an array of microprocessors that control a myriad of car functions: fuel injection, ignition timing, transmission shifting, suspension, braking, power steering, and even the air bags. They may be more confusing for mechanics, but for the rest of us the chips mean a smoother and safer ride.

QUALITY

TOWARD A MORE PERFECT CHIP

Chips are known to be reliable; that is because they are rigorously tested and given a strong go/no-go test. But few chips make it that far. In fact, as originally produced, most chips do not work and are thrown out. The problem? Despite clean rooms, there is imperfect silicon, faulty design, etching misalignments, and foreign matter such as hair and dirt.

Execution time ____________________

Firmware ____________________

Gigabyte (GB) ____________________

Instruction time ____________________

Internal storage ____________________

I-time ____________________

K ____________________

Kilobyte (KB) ____________________

Logic chip ____________________

Logical operations ____________________

Machine cycle ____________________

Main memory ______________________

Main storage ______________________

Megabyte (MB) ______________________

Megaflop ______________________

Megahertz ______________________

Memory ______________________

Microprocessor ______________________

Microsecond ______________________

Millisecond ______________________

MIPS ______________________

Nanosecond ______________________

Parallel processing ______________________

Parity bit ______________________

Picosecond ______________________

Pipelining ______________________

Primary memory ______________________

Primary storage ______________________

PROM ______________________

RAM ______________________

Register ______________________

RISC ______________________

ROM ______________________

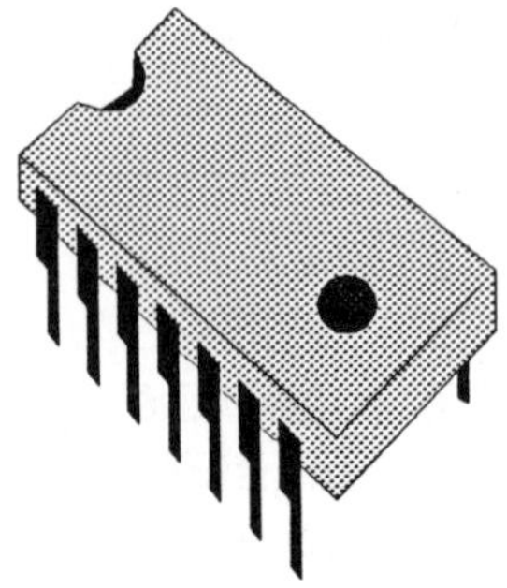

Semiconductor storage ______________

____

____

Serial processing ________________

____

____

SIMM ________________________

____

____

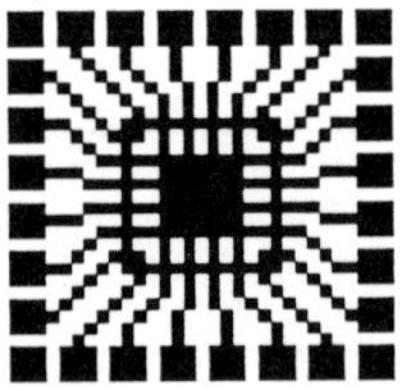

Static RAM (SRAM) _____________

____

____

Storage register ________________

____

____

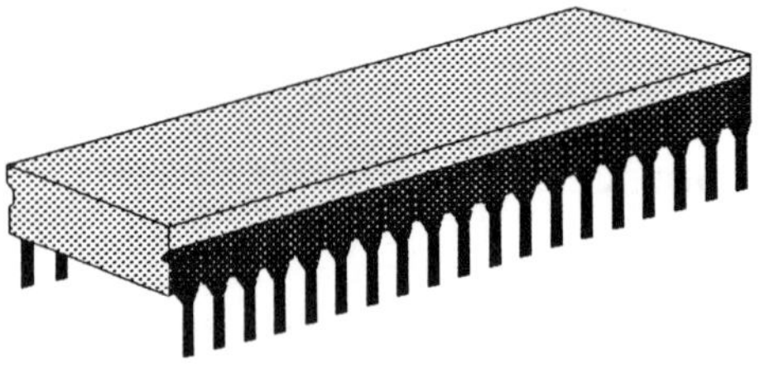

Unicode ______________________

____

____

Word ________________________

____

____

Study Hints

The material in this chapter is somewhat abstract and therefore somewhat more difficult than the other chapters. However, it is critical that you understand the material in this chapter; the central processing unit operations are the essence of computing.

Study the chapter carefully before the lecture and then be prepared to ask questions of your instructor, to clear up any murky areas.

Self-Test

Multiple Choice

1. The complex set of electrical circuitry that executes program instructions is called the
   a. register
   b. accumulator
   c. central processing unit
   d. bus line

2. The entire computer system is coordinated by
   a. the ALU
   b. the control unit
   c. the accumulator
   d. arithmetic operators

3. A bus line consists of
   a. registers
   b. parallel data lines
   c. accumulators
   d. machine cycles

4. Equal to, less than, and greater than are examples of
   a. logical operations
   b. subtraction
   c. locations
   d. arithmetic operations

5. The primary storage unit is also known as
   a. storage registers
   b. mass storage
   c. accumulators
   d. memory

6. Data and instructions are put into primary storage by
   a. memory
   b. secondary storage
   c. the control unit
   d. the ALU

7. Registers that collect the results of computations are
   a. general-purpose
   b. storage registers
   c. main storage
   d. accumulators

8. During E-time, the ALU
   a. examines the instruction
   b. executes the instruction
   c. enters the instruction
   d. elicits the instruction

9. When the control unit gets an instruction it is called
   a. E-time
   b. I-time
   c. machine time
   d. ALU time

10. When the control unit directs the ALU to perform an operation on the data, the machine cycle is involved in its
    a. first step
    b. second step
    c. third step
    d. fourth step

11. Computer operations are synchronized by
    a. the CPU clock
    b. the binary system
    c. megabytes
    d. E-time

12. Another name for primary storage is
    a. secondary storage
    b. firmware
    c. ROM
    d. main storage

13. Which is NOT another name for memory:
    a. primary storage
    b. internal storage
    c. main storage
    d. secondary storage

14. Another name for a logic chip is
    a. PROM
    b. microprocessor
    c. memory
    d. firmware

15. Data is represented on a computer by means of a two-state on/off system called
    a. a bit
    b. a byte
    c. the binary system
    d. RAM

16. A letter, number, or character is represented by a
    a. bit
    b. byte
    c. kilobyte
    d. megabyte

17. Memory capacity may be expressed in
    a. microseconds
    b. bits
    c. kilobytes
    d. cycles

18. Which is NOT a kind of register:
    a. storage
    b. accumulator
    c. address
    d. variable

19. A commonly used coding scheme that uses eight bits to represent a character is
    a. LSI
    b. ASCII
    c. EBCDIC
    d. VLSI

20. A bit that is added to the byte as a check is called a
a. parity bit
b. gigabyte
c. word
d. tenth bit

21. The data coding scheme that is the American standard is
a. ASCII
b. SIMM
c. KB
d. EBCDIC

22. Tools to change PROM chips are called
a. chip kits
b. PROM burners
c. RAM burners
d. none of these

23. An approach to increase speed is
a. Unicode
b. serial processing
c. parallel processing
d. parity

24. The shortest period of time is a
a. millisecond
b. picosecond
c. nanosecond
d. microsecond

25. An organic chip is called a:
a. storage chip
b. microchip
c. biochip
d. silicon chip

True/False

T F 1. The control unit consists of the CPU and the ALU.

T F 2. Secondary storage holds data only temporarily.

T F 3. The control unit directs and coordinates the entire computer system in executing stored program instructions with electrical signals.

T F 4. A microcomputer has a 16-bit word and 64 parallel data bus lines.

T F 5. The electronic circuitry that controls all arithmetic and logical operations is contained in the ALU.

T F 6. The three basic logical operations may be combined to form a total of nine commonly used operations.

T F 7. Memory allows very fast access to instructions in secondary storage.

T F **8.** Registers are temporary storage areas located in memory.

T F **9.** Address registers hold the addresses of locations containing data needed for an instruction.

T F **10.** RISC technology uses fewer instructions than traditional computers.

T F **11.** All computers except microcomputers can execute more than one instruction at a time.

T F **12.** The machine cycle consists of four steps, from the first step of fetching the instructions to the last step of placing the result of the operation into memory.

T F **13.** The internal clock of the CPU produces pulses at a fixed rate to synchronize all computer operations.

T F **14.** Unicode uses just a single digit.

T F **15.** Computers represent all data using a two-state on/off system called the binary system.

T F **16.** A bit is commonly made of seven or eight bytes.

T F **17.** A kilobyte (KB) is 1024 bytes.

T F **18.** A computer word is defined as the number of bits constituting a common unit of information for a specific computer system.

T F **19.** Another name for memory is secondary storage.

T F **20.** Serial processing is replacing parallel processing.

T F **21.** Addition and subtraction are logical operations.

T F **22.** Primary storage is part of the central processing unit.

T F **23.** Memory is usually volatile.

T F **24.** A microsecond is briefer than a millisecond.

T F **25.** The ASCII coding scheme is accepted as the American standard.

Matching I

___	1. executes instructions	a.	control unit
___	2. accumulator	b.	ROM
___	3. bit	c.	serial processing
___	4. firmware	d.	CPU
___	5. machine cycle	e.	binary digit
___	6. directs and coordinates	f.	KB
___	7. data transfer	g.	primary storage unit
___	8. 1024 bytes	h.	I-time plus E-time
___	9. one instruction at a time	i.	register
___	10. internal storage	j.	bus line

Matching II

___	1. fewer instructions	a.	control unit
___	2. logical operation	b.	address
___	3. ASCII	c.	gigabyte
___	4. part of CPU	d.	greater than
___	5. parity bit	e.	memory
___	6. arithmetic operation	f.	subtraction
___	7. memory location	g.	standard code
___	8. main storage	h.	logic chip
___	9. billions of bytes	i.	RISC
___	10. microprocessor	j.	check bit

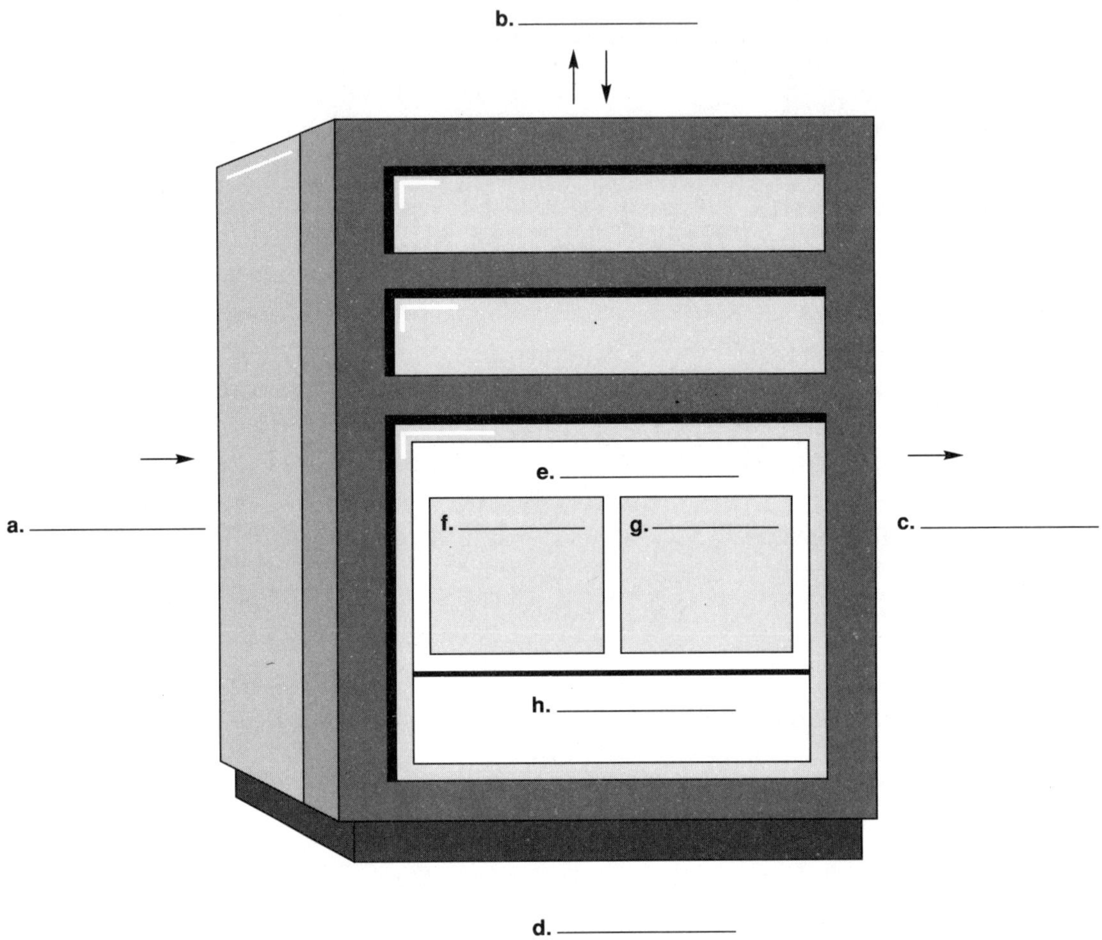

Figure 1 The central processing unit.

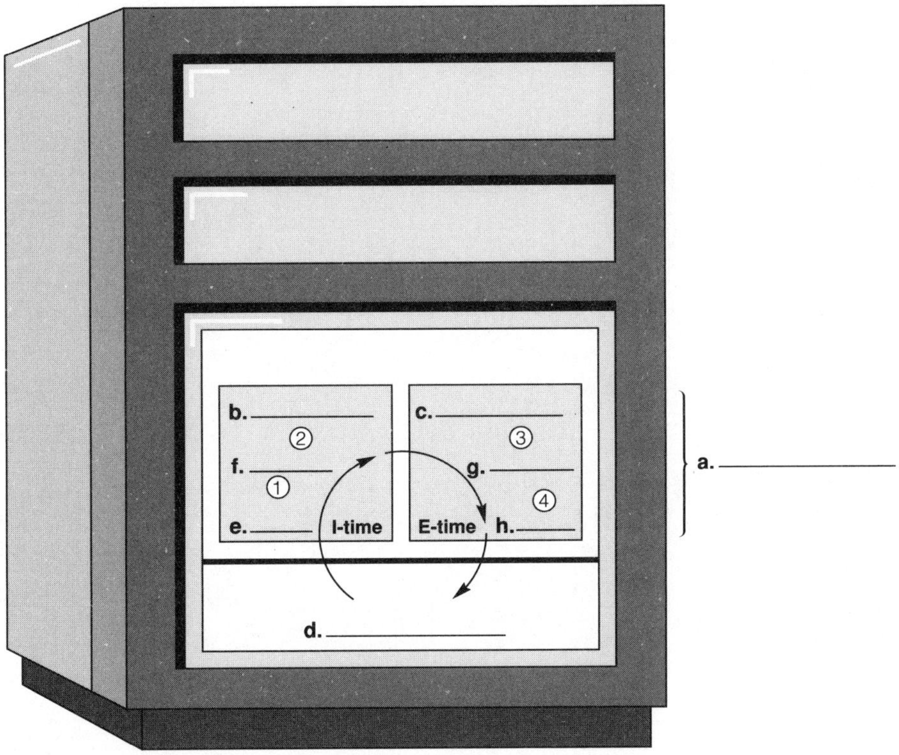

Figure 2 The machine cycle.

Fill-In

1. What is a millionth of a second called? 1. ____________

2. What is the unit that consists of both the control unit and the arithmetic/logic unit? 2. ____________

3. Name the four kinds of arithmetic operations performed by the ALU.
3.a. ____________
b. ____________
c. ____________
d. ____________

4. List five other names for memory.
4.a. ____________
b. ____________
c. ____________
d. ____________
e. ____________

5. Which type of register is used for both arithmetic and addressing purposes? 5. ____________

6. What is the abbreviation for memory chips that can be altered? 6. ____________

7. What is a combination of I-time and E-time called? 7. ____________

8. A possible future code to store all the world's languages: 8. ____________

9. How is the location in memory of each instruction identified? 9. ____________

10. What is each 0 or 1 in the binary system called?	**10.**	____________
11. How many bits for each character are used by ASCII?	**11.**	____________
12. Name a disadvantage of semiconductor storage.	**12.**	____________
13. A data path to transfer data:	**13.**	____________
14. What does RAM stand for?	**14.**	____________
15. What is another term for ROM?	**15.**	____________
16. Which type of storage stores programs that will not be altered?	**16.**	____________
17. Which register holds information taken from or sent to memory?	**17.**	____________
18. What are the comparing operations called that are controlled by the ALU?	**18.**	____________
19. What are many processors working at the same time called?	**19.**	____________
20. When the control unit decodes an instruction, is the machine cycle in I-time or E-time?	**20.**	____________
21. What does RISC stand for?	**21.**	____________
22. What does CMOS stand for?	**22.**	____________
23. Processing instructions one at a time is called:	**23.**	____________
24. The two digits of the binary system:	**24.**	____________
25. IBM's data coding scheme is:	**25.**	____________

Test Answers

Multiple Choice

1. c	6. c	11. a	16. b	21. a
2. b	7. d	12. d	17. c	22. d
3. b	8. b	13. c	18. d	23. d
4. a	9. b	14. b	19. c	24. b
5. d	10. c	15. c	20. a	25. c

True/False

1. F	6. F	11. F	16. F	21. F
2. F	7. F	12. T	17. T	22. F
3. T	8. F	13. T	18. T	23. T
4. F	9. T	14. F	19. F	24. T
5. T	10. T	15. T	20. F	25. T

Matching I

1. d	6. a
2. i	7. j
3. e	8. f
4. b	9. c
5. h	10. g

Matching II

1. i	6. f
2. d	7. b
3. g	8. e
4. a	9. c
5. j	10. h

Figures

Figure 1
a. input
b. secondary storage
c. output
d. processing
e. central processing unit
f. control unit
g. arithmetic/logic unit
h. memory

Figure 2
a. central processing unit
b. control unit
c. arithmetic/logic unit
d. memory
e. fetch
f. decode
g. execute
h. store

Fill-In

1. microsecond
2. central processing unit
3. a. addition, b. subtraction, c. multiplication, d. division
4. a. main storage
   b. internal storage
   c. primary storage
   d. primary memory
   e. main memory
5. general-purpose register
6. PROM
7. a machine cycle
8. Unicode
9. an address
10. a bit
11. seven
12. it's volatile
13. bus line
14. random-access memory
15. firmware
16. ROM
17. storage register
18. logical operations
19. parallel processing
20. I-time
21. Reduced Instruction Set Computer
22. Complementary metal oxide semiconductor
23. serial processing
24. 0 and 1
25. EBCDIC

Close to Home

If you have your own personal computer at home you will, of course, have a processor as the heart of that system. But that does not mean you will be paying much attention to it. The processor requires nothing from you in the way of maintenance.

Since we can take the CPU for granted, let us consider, instead, the mighty microprocessor as a tool of daily living. Can you imagine a machine in your home that could *not* be controlled by a chip planted in its innards? You already know about watches and ovens that are controlled by microprocessors; it is only a small leap in the imagination to include dishwashers, lamps, refrigerators, heaters, and just about any device you have in your home.

CHAPTER

3

Input and Output: Data Given, Information Received

Learning Objectives

- ❑ Appreciating the various forms of input for computer systems.
- ❑ Understanding how data is input to a computer system and appreciating the advantages and disadvantages of each method.
- ❑ Recognizing that some devices are used for both input and output.
- ❑ Understanding the difference between impact and nonimpact printers and becoming familiar with the various kinds.

Why This Chapter Is Important

Input and output represent the people connection with computers. The process of transmitting data from people to machines begins with the concept of input. As a computer user, even in an indirect sense, you will be providing input to the computer for the rest of your life. This chapter should give you the flavor of the many approaches to the input process. In addition, you should understand how data that started out as the raw material of human activity - names, test scores, money owed, and so forth - is translated into a form that the computer can accept and use.

Improved input methods are a primary challenge for the computer industry; think of all those people who do not type. Or, more simply, think of yourself and all the rest of us who would like to be able to communicate with the computer in a way that seems more natural, like just talking or looking. Some forms of these methods are available now, but they are far from being sophisticated.

Output is used directly by people, which, of course, is its attraction. Although paper is still a major form of output, the more dramatic forms are getting attention in the media.

Chapter Outline

Input and Output: The People Connection

The Forms of Input

Types of Input
- Keyboard Entry
  - Keyboards and Personal Computer Users
  - Keyboards and Data Entry Operators
- The Mouse
- Source Data Automation: Collecting Data Where It Starts
  - Magnetic-Ink Character Recognition
  - Optical Recognition
    - Optical-Mark Recognition
    - Optical-Character Recognition
    - Handwritten Characters
    - Bar Codes
  - Data Collection Devices
  - Voice Input

Computer Screens: Input/Output Devices
- CRT Screen Technology
- Terminals
- Pen-Based Computers and Interactive Tablets

Types of Output
- Printers: The Image Makers
  - Impact Printers
  - Nonimpact Printers
  - Which Type of Printer?
  - Paper
- Computer Output Microfilm
- Voice Output: Your Master's (Digital) Voice

Yet To Come

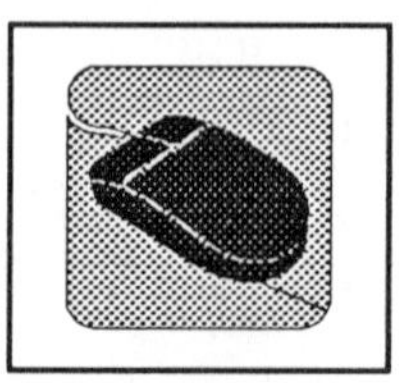

Key Words

Audio-response unit ____________________

Backlighting ____________________

Band printer ____________________

Bar code ____________________

Bar code reader ____________________

Bit-mapped display ____________________

Bursting ____________________

Cathode ray tube (CRT) ____________________

Chain printer ____________________

Character printer ____________________

Computer output microfilm (COM) ____________________

Continuous word systems ____________________

Cursor ____________________

Daisy wheel printer ____________________

Data collection device ____________________

Data entry operator ____________________

Decollating ____________________

Discrete word systems ____________________

Dot-addressable display ____________________

Dot-matrix printer ____________________

Double-click

Drum printer

Dumb terminal

Flat-panel display

GIGO

Green-bar paper

Hard copy

Icon

Impact printer

Ink-jet printer

Inquiry

Intelligent terminal

Interactive tablet

Laser printer

Line printer

Liquid crystal display (LCD)

Magnetic-ink character recognition

MICR inscriber

MICR reader/sorter

Microfiche

Monochrome screen

Mouse

NCR paper ______________________

____

Nonimpact printer ______________________

____

Notepad computer ______________________

____

Optical recognition ______________________

____

Optical-character recognition (OCR)

____

Optical-mark recognition (OMR) ____

____

Pen-based computer ______________________

____

Pixel ______________________

____

Pointer ______________________

____

Point-of-sale terminal (POS) ________

____

Printer ______________________

____

Prompt ______________________

____

Raster scan ______________________

____

Refreshed screen ______________________

____

Resolution ______________________

____

Scan rate ______________________

____

Smart terminal ______________________

____

Source data automation ____________

____

Source document ______________________

____

Speech recognition ______________________

____

Speech synthesis ______________________

____

Stock tab paper ______________________

____

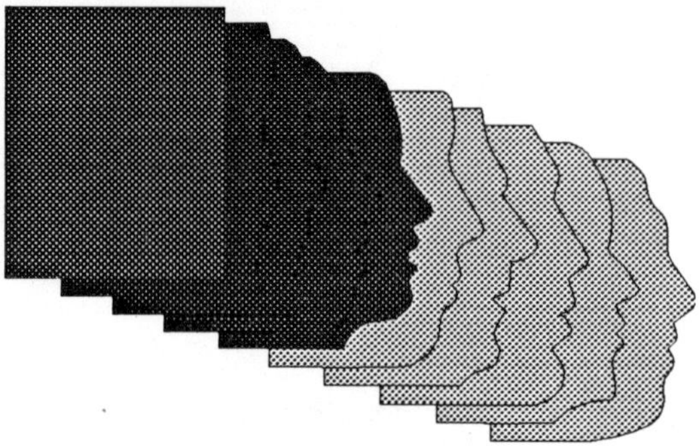

ONE FACE FROM MANY

You have probably seen an artist's rendition of a suspect sought by the police: A police artist makes the drawing to match the description provided by the victim. This is a useful but limited technique because most people have difficulty describing facial characteristics. But what if the victim could see samples of facial characteristics - bobbed nose, squinty eyes, sunken cheeks - and simply point to the ones that seem to fit? Now take this a step further by combining the various characteristics into one face. This process could be done manually, but a new computer technique makes it significantly faster and more effective.

Technology developed by M.I.T lets a victim create a composite picture of a suspect interactively. Sample faces are displayed, one after another, on a color screen. The victim presses a button whenever a face is reminiscent of the suspect. When several faces have been selected, the computer presents a composite face, which is then used to help catch the criminal.

Synthesis by analysis ____________________

Synthesis by rule ____________________

Trackball ____________________

Universal Product Code (UPC) ____________________

Video display terminal ____________________

Voice input ____________________

Voice output ____________________

Voice synthesizer ____________________

Wand reader ____________________

Study Hints

Study the forms of input by category. Which require intermediate processing steps? Which fall under the classification source data automation? Categorize output choices by the needs of the user.

Self-Test

Multiple Choice

1. Computer output produced as small film images is called
   a. OCR
   b. LCD
   c. COM
   d. OMR

2. A small screen figure that represents a computer activity is called a(n)
   a. pointer
   b. icon
   c. touch screen
   d. MICR

3. The removal of carbon paper from standard multiple forms is called
   a. bursting
   b. decollating
   c. detailing
   d. rolling

4. One type of character printer useful for professional correspondence is a
   a. drum printer
   b. line printer
   c. daisy wheel printer
   d. band printer

5. The impact printer that consists of a cylinder with embossed rows of characters is a
   a. chain printer
   b. drum printer
   c. character printer
   d. band printer

6. An ink-jet printer is an example of a(n)
   a. daisy wheel printer
   b. impact printer
   c. drum printer
   d. nonimpact printer

7. Entering data into the system as a by-product of the activity that generates the data is called
   a. source data automation
   b. a discrete word system
   c. optical-character recognition
   d. MICR entry

8. The rate of screen refreshment is called
   a. pixel speed
   b. bit-map speed
   c. raster rate
   d. scan rate

9. Magnetic characters are produced on your bank checks by
   a. bar code readers
   b. mice
   c. MICR inscribers
   d. microfiche

10. "Mark sensing" is another term for
a. MICR
b. POS
c. OMR
d. bit-mapping

11. A device used for optical-character recognition is a
a. wand reader
b. cursor
c. pen
d. MICR reader

12. OCR-A is a(n)
a. intelligent terminal
b. standard typeface
c. wand reader
d. bar code

13. POS terminals are similar to
a. calculators
b. touch-tone telephones
c. UPCs
d. cash registers

14. A one-color screen on a black background is called
a. monochrome
b. blank
c. dot addressable
d. liquid crystal display

15. Voice input devices convert voice input to
a. digital codes
b. bar codes
c. OCR-A
d. optical marks

16. When the computer, through the screen, requests information from the user, this is called a(n)
a. inquiry
b. prompt
c. icon
d. request

17. The cursor can be moved by an imbedded ball called a
a. mouse
b. trackball
c. wand reader
d. interactive tablet

18. A CRT screen location may be moved by a computer input device called a(n)
a. mouse
b. graphic display
c. cursor
d. MICR inscriber device

19. A display lighter and slimmer than a CRT is
a. COM
b. graphics card
c. flat panel
d. terminal

20. A knob that allows fingertip control of figures on a CRT screen is called a(n)
a. pixel
b. cursor
c. trackball
d. mouse

21. Another name for a pen-based computer is
a. smart terminal
b. COM
c. MICR inscriber
d. interactive tablet

22. The acronym that means the quality of output depends on the quality of the input is
a. GIGO
b. NCR
c. OMR
d. LCD

23. A bar code represents the product's
a. ATM
b. OMR
c. LCD
d. UPC

24. A printer that forms characters from a series of dots is called
a. dot-matrix
b. band
c. character
d. drum

25. A paper that can be used as an alternative to carbon paper is
a. monochrome
b. green-bar
c. microfiche
d. NCR

True/False

T F 1. The greater the number of pixels, the poorer the screen clarity.

T F 2. Stock tab paper and green-bar paper are two examples of paper that might come off a printer.

T F 3. Smart terminals can be programmed by the user to do a variety of tasks.

T F 4. Discrete word voice input systems allow a normal rate of speaking.

T F 5. Nonimpact printers can make carbon copies.

T F 6. A pen-based computer is also called a notepad computer.

T F 7. CRT stands for computer remote terminal.

T F 8. Optical recognition may be categorized according to optical marks, optical characters, handwritten characters, and bar codes.

T F 9. OMR senses marks on paper.

T F 10. A wand reader can read OCR characters.

T F 11. Dumb terminals can process, but not store, data.

T F 12. A prompt occurs when the computer requests information from the user.

T F 13. LCD stands for liquid crystal display.

T F 14. COM can be read directly by a computer.

T F 15. A mouse can be double clicked.

T F 16. The MICR process is used mainly by stores for processing purchases.

T F 17. A cursor is an indicator on a screen that shows where the next character will be inserted.

T F 18. Handwritten characters can never be used for data entry because of their general lack of uniformity.

T F 19. COM can be produced on either 35mm film or microfiche.

T F 20. Means of input are distinct from, and unrelated to, means of output.

T F 21. Pixel stands for picture element.

T F 22. Checkout at the supermarket is usually faster with a UPC system.

T F 23. Optical marks are sometimes used to record test answers.

T F 24. Nonimpact printers are quieter than impact printers.

T F 25. Laser printers use a light beam to transfer images to paper.

Matching I

___	1. picture element	a. OCR-A
___	2. mark-sense forms	b. inquiry
___	3. wand reader	c. bar codes
___	4. dot addressable	d. OCR
___	5. standard typeface	e. pixel
___	6. mouse	f. interactive tablet
___	7. backlighting	g. on wheels
___	8. request to computer	h. flat panel
___	9. notepad computer	i. OMR
___	10. Universal Product Code	j. bit mapped

Matching II

___	1. laser printer	a. picture symbol
___	2. icon	b. monochrome
___	3. voice input	c. microfiche
___	4. data collection devices	d. audio response
___	5. double click	e. fastest, quietest
___	6. cursor	f. speech recognition
___	7. one color	g. pointer
___	8. voice synthesizer	h. mouse
___	9. character printer	i. factories
___	10. COM	j. daisy wheel

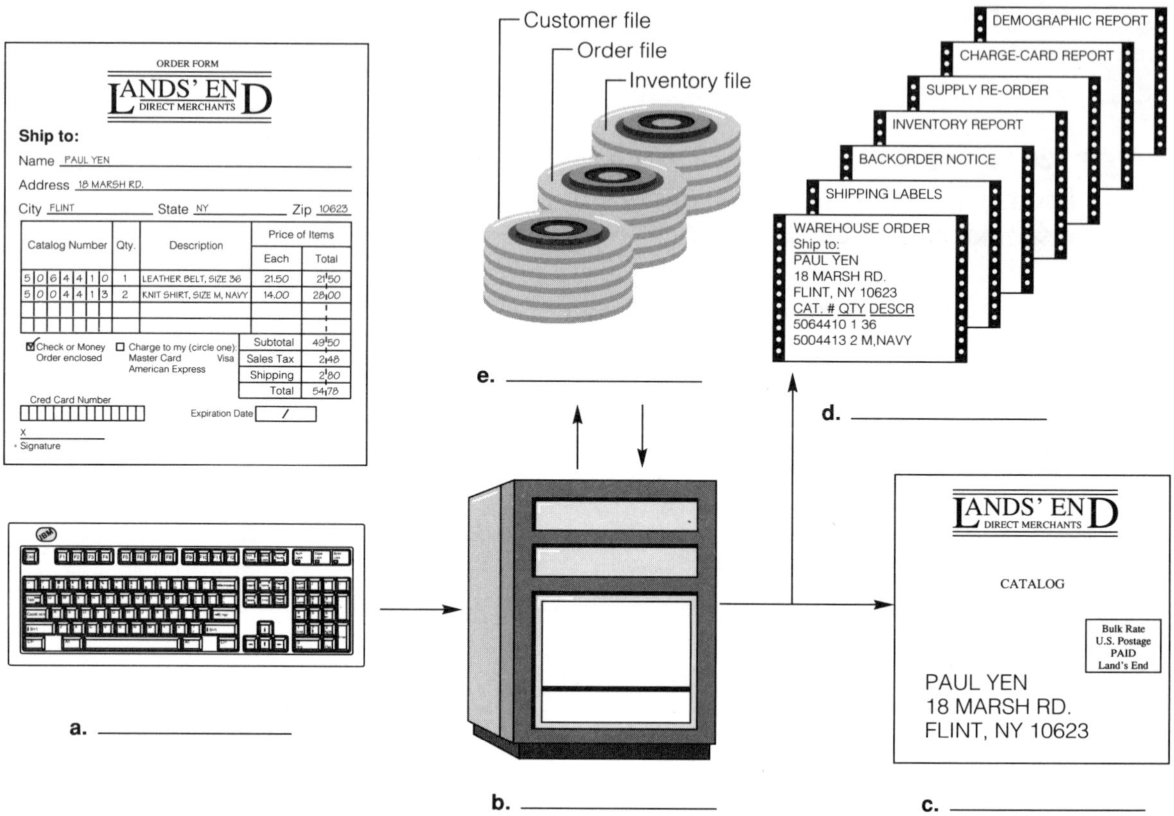

Figure 1 Lands' End: Input, processing, and output

Fill-In

1. What does GIGO stand for?	1.	________________
2. What does LCD stand for?	2.	________________
3. From what do data entry operators enter large amounts of data?	3.	________________
4. What is the term that describes the separation of continuous paper that has been fed through the printer?	4.	________________
5. What do the letters *NCR* of NCR paper stand for?	5.	________________
6. What are the two general categories of impact printers?	6.a.	________________
	b.	________________
7. What are three examples of impact line printers?	7.a.	________________
	b.	________________
	c.	________________
8. What phrase is used to describe the use of special equipment to collect data at the source and send it to the computer?	8.	________________
9. What does UPC stand for?	9.	________________
10. Which method is used mainly by banks for processing checks?	10.	________________
11. What is the general term for systems that use electronic scanners to read numbers, letters, special characters, and marks?	11.	________________

12. What method uses a light beam to sense marks on machine-readable test forms? 12. ____________

13. What is the term for the 4" x 6" sheets of film used for COM? 13. ____________

14. Which technology is more advanced, voice input or voice output? 14. ____________

15. What kind of terminal can read bar codes and is like a cash register in many ways? 15. ____________

16. What is screen output called? 16. ____________

17. What is printed computer output called? 17. ____________

18. A terminal that can only enter data and receive output is called: 18. ____________

19. What is the name for the input device used in graphic display that one rolls to move the screen location? 19. ____________

20. What is the system in which the computer analyzes stored tapes of spoken words? 20. ____________

21. The number of times a screen is refreshed is called its 21. ____________

22. VDT stands for 22. ____________

23. The Universal Product Code is represented on a package by a 23. ____________

24. A speech recognition system limited to isolated words is called 24. ____________

25. Screen clarity is called 25. ____________

Test Answers

Multiple Choice

1. c	6. d	11. a	16. b	21. d
2. b	7. a	12. b	17. b	22. a
3. b	8. d	13. d	18. a	23. d
4. c	9. c	14. a	19. c	24. a
5. b	10. c	15. a	20. c	25. d

True/False

1. F	6. T	11. F	16. F	21. T
2. T	7. F	12. T	17. T	22. T
3. F	8. T	13. T	18. F	23. T
4. F	9. T	14. F	19. T	24. T
5. F	10. T	15. T	20. F	25. T

Matching I

1. e	6. g
2. i	7. h
3. d	8. b
4. j	9. f
5. a	10. c

Matching II

1. e	6. g
2. a	7. b
3. f	8. d
4. i	9. j
5. h	10. c

Figure

Figure 1
a. input
b. processing
c. output
d. output
e. secondary storage

Fill-In

1. garbage in, garbage out
2. liquid crystal display
3. source documents
4. bursting
5. no carbon required
6. a. line
   b. character
7. a. band
   b. drum
   c. chain
8. source data automation
9. Universal Product Code
10. MICR
11. optical recognition
12. OMR
13. microfiche
14. voice output
15. POS terminal
16. soft copy
17. hard copy
18. dumb terminal
19. mouse
20. synthesis by analysis
21. scan rate
22. video display terminal
23. bar code
24. discrete word system
25. resolution

LONGEST AND SHORTEST

The world's longest bar code: 375 feet long, placed around the base of California's Palomar Observatory to indicate dome positioning.

The world's shortest bar code: 2.8 millimeters, applied to bees' thoraxes with shellac to monitor behavior.

Close to Home

One way or another, delivering input to the computer is a common activity in our daily lives. Let's take a quick survey of input activities in which you may have engaged in recent days and weeks. Check yourself out on the following list. Have you

- ✓ Bought an item whose price tag was scanned with a wand reader?
- ✓ Filled out an application for a magazine subscription?
- ✓ Purchased groceries whose bar codes were scanned?
- ✓ Filled out registration forms?
- ✓ Recorded test answers using a pencil on an OMR sheet?

The preceding items are pretty routine. There are many other activities that require us to provide input to the computer. Over a period of time, many of us supply input in these circumstances: entering the hospital, seeking credit, paying taxes, applying for a job, entering a contest, paying bills, entering the armed services, signing a petition, joining an organization, applying for a scholarship or grant, seeking government assistance, giving charitable donations, ordering products through the mail, and on and on.

This data is supplied willingly, and most people give little thought to the route it will travel. Almost all of the data will end up on a computer file, to reside there indefinitely. The consideration of the files themselves is another topic; for now, be aware that it all starts with input.

Now consider the computer output that is all around us. Sometimes it is not obvious. You have received computer-produced bills and have doubtless learned to spot personalized computer junk mail. ("We can send this product right to your home at 5738 4th Avenue. . .") But some mail is fully automated and not at all obvious; it looks like a nicely-typed letter and even has an inked signature on it.

TELLING IT WHERE TO GO

Where does your luggage go when it disappears into a black hole after you check it at the airport? It goes where it is told to go, literally, using a voice recognition system. As each bag, tagged with its destination, passes by, a baggage handler reads the tag and utters the name of the city into the computer voice input system. As the bag progresses along the main conveyer belt line, the computer monitors its progress.

CHAPTER

4

Storage Devices and File Processing: Electronic Facts

Learning Objectives

- ❑ Understanding the need for secondary storage.
- ❑ Understanding how data is organized and processed.
- ❑ Understanding the principal types of secondary storage, magnetic tape and magnetic disk, and their advantages and disadvantages.
- ❑ Understanding three methods of file organization: sequential, direct, and indexed sequential.
- ❑ Understanding the storage media available for personal computers.
- ❑ Appreciating new approaches to storage media, particularly optical technology.

Why This Chapter Is Important

This chapter lays the foundation for concepts that are of critical importance to a career as a programmer or systems analyst. Understanding how to organize and access data is just as important as learning to write the programs that will use the data.

However, even a casual computer user will benefit by knowing how the computer stores and retrieves data.

PAYING FOR WHAT YOU USE

CD-ROM disks can hold vast amounts of data, even an entire encyclopedia. That makes them pretty expensive for the average customer. But now new technology is solving the problem: a meter gauges data use in much the same way a meter keeps track of the electricity you use in your home. The user is charged for only the data used, a considerable reduction.

Chapter Outline

ADMISSION BY DISKETTE

If you have ever applied to a dozen colleges and filled out a different form for each one, you can appreciate the efficiency of applying to all of them with just one application - on disk. CollegeLink, of Concord, Mass., convinced over 200 colleges to make their forms identical. The student sends the completed disk application to CollegeLink, which sends paper copies to the appropriate schools.

Key Words

Access arm ______________________

Auxiliary storage ______________________

Backup system ______________________

Batch processing ______________________

Block ______________________

Blocking factor ______________________

Bytes per inch (bpi) ______________________

Cache ______________________

Channel ______________________

Character ______________________

Characters per inch (cpi) ______________________

Compact disk read-only memory ______________________

CD-ROM ______________________

Cylinder ______________________

Data compression ______________________

Data transfer ______________________

Density ______________________

Digital audio tape ______________________

Direct access ______________________

Direct-access storage device (DASD) ______________________

Direct file processing ______________________________

Disk drive ______________________________

Disk pack ______________________________

Diskette ______________________________

Erasable optical disk ______________________________

Erase head ______________________________

Field ______________________________

File ______________________________

Flash memory ______________________________

Hardcard ______________________________

Hard disk ______________________________

Hashing ______________________________

Head switching ______________________________

Helical scan recording ______________________________

Hit rate ______________________________

Indexed file processing ______________________________

Interactive ______________________________

Interblock gap (IBG) ______________________________

Interrecord gap (IRG) ______________________________

Key ______________________________

Logical record ______________________________

Magnetic disk ______________________________

Magnetic tape ______________________

Master file ______________________

On-line ______________________

Optical read-only memory (OROM) __

Physical record ______________________

RAM disk ______________________

Random access ______________________

Randomizing ______________________

Read/write head ______________________

Real-time processing ______________________

Record ______________________

Rotational delay ______________________

Secondary storage ______________________

Sector method ______________________

Seek time ______________________

Sequential file processing ______________________

Sort ______________________

Supply reel ______________________

Take-up reel ______________________

Time-sharing ______________________

TAKE ME OFF YOUR MAILING LIST!

Tired of getting junk mail? Of course, you can always write directly to all those institutions you do business with and ask not to be included on any mailing lists they lease or lend. But just think of all those files you are on!

You can write to the Direct Mail Marketing Association (6 East 43rd Street, New York, NY 10017) and request that a so-called "mail preference form" be sent to you free of charge. When you return the form, it will be circulated to hundreds of mail-order houses and other institutions. After a few months your unsolicited mail should diminish. The same form can be used to get more mail-order advertising if you check off any category of merchandise of interest to you.

Track ____________________

Transaction file ____________________

Transaction processing ____________________

Update ____________________

Winchester technology ____________________

Winnie ____________________

Write-once, read-only (WORM) disk ____________________

Zone recording ____________________

Study Hints

Try to get a first hand look at the hardware discussed in this chapter. It should not be difficult to find the storage media for personal computers; they are available in many places including your school and local retail outlets. Less accessible, but even more useful, are full-size disk packs. The concepts presented in the chapter are much easier to understand if a disk pack is in view.

Self-Test

Multiple Choice

1. The amount of data that can be stored on magnetic tape is expressed through the number of
   a. units per inch
   b. tracks per inch
   c. channels per inch
   d. bytes per inch

2. On most computer tapes, one cross section of the tape has one bit on each
   a. of the seven channels
   b. byte
   c. of the nine tracks
   d. character

3. A magnetized spot represents a
   a. cpi
   b. 0 bit
   c. bpi
   d. 1 bit

4. A field contains one or more
   a. characters
   b. databases
   c. records
   d. files

5. The reel that is changed on a magnetic tape unit is the
   a. take-up reel
   b. block
   c. supply reel
   d. end-of-file record

6. Hard disk can be backed up efficiently using
   a. blocks
   b. tape backup system
   c. RAM disks
   d. diskettes

7. Relatively permanent data is contained in
   a. a field
   b. memory
   c. a transaction
   d. a master file

8. A disadvantage of magnetic tape as a method of storing data is that it is
   a. not reusable
   b. organized sequentially
   c. relatively expensive
   d. not portable

9. An example of a direct-access storage device is
   a. disk storage
   b. tape storage
   c. a mass storage device
   d. all of these

10. Optical disk technology uses a
   a. RAM chip
   b. hardcard
   c. laser beam
   d. magnetic field

11. The mechanism for reading or writing data on a disk is called a(n)
   a. track
   b. channel
   c. key
   d. access arm

12. A disk pack within a sealed data module is a
   a. backup unit
   b. diskette
   c. Winnie
   d. CD-ROM

13. The time required for the access arm to get into position over a particular track is
   a. rotational delay
   b. seek time
   c. data transfer
   d. head switching

14. A way of physically organizing data on a disk pack to minimize seek time uses
   a. sequential file
   b. the cylinder method
   c. fixed-length recording organization
   d. Winchester technology

15. Direct file processing is also known as
   a. random access
   b. sequential file
   c. indexed file processing
   d. sector method processing

16. OROM media are
   a. read/write
   b. write only
   c. read only
   d. read once

17. A RAM disk is really a(n)
   a. CD-ROM
   b. optical disk
   c. chip
   d. hardcard

18. Before a sequential file can be updated the transactions must first be
   a. numbered
   b. sorted
   c. labeled
   d. updated

19. Hashing, to get an address, is the process of applying a formula to a
   a. key
   b. file
   c. record
   d. block

20. The stopping space between records on a magnetic tape is called the
    a. key
    b. block
    c. end-of-file record
    d. interblock gap

21. CD-ROM has the same format as a(an)
    a. tape
    b. diskettes
    c. hardcard
    d. audio compact disk

22. If the blocking factor is 5 and the physical record is 2000 bytes then the block has how many bytes?
    a. 400
    b. 50
    c. 2000
    d. 10000

23. If the blocking factor is 5 and the physical record is 2000 bytes then the logical record has how many bytes?
    a. 400
    b. 50
    c. 2000
    d. 10000

24. If the blocking factor is 5 and the logical record is 2000 bytes then the block has how many bytes?
    a. 400
    b. 50
    c. 2000
    d. 10000

25. If the blocking factor is 5 and the logical record is 2000 bytes then the physical record has how many bytes?
    a. 400
    b. 50
    c. 2000
    d. 10000

True/False

T F 1. Real-time processing gives results fast enough to affect the activity using the computer system.

T F 2. Processing data by groups of transactions is called batch processing.

T F 3. A 0 bit is represented on magnetic tape by a magnetized spot.

T F 4. A magnetic tape unit records data on tape but cannot retrieve it.

T F 5. A transaction file contains records to update the master file.

T F 6. WORM can be written once; then it becomes read-only.

T F 7. Rotational delay comes before seek time.

T F 8. Density is the number of character per inch.

T F 9. The quickest way to back up hard disk is onto diskettes.

T F 10. Another name for OROM is hardcard.

T F 11. Transaction processing systems are usually time-sharing systems.

T F 12. A physical record is also known as a block.

T F 13. A drawback of magnetic tape is it sequentially organized.

T F 14. Optical disk can never be erased.

T F 15. Each magnetic disk has concentric tracks designed to hold the same amount of data as every other track on the disk.

T F 16. "The blocking factor is three" means there are three physical records in a logical record.

T F 17. The cylinder method is a means of physically organizing data on a disk pack horizontally to minimize seek time.

T F 18. Direct file organization is a combination of sequential and indexed file organization.

T F 19. Zone recording takes full advantage of the space on a disk track.

T F 20. Hashing is a process used to locate records sequentially.

T F 21. Data compression is a method of backing up data.

T F 22. A field is a set of related records.

T F 23. Auxiliary storage can be used only temporarily.

T F 24. A database is a collection of interrelated records.

T F 25. Indexed records are stored in sequential order.

Matching

___	1. real-time processing	a.	concentric
___	2. interrecord gap	b.	randomizing
___	3. magnetic disk	c.	IBG
___	4. sealed data module	d.	channel
___	5. sequential file	e.	physical record
___	6. hashing	f.	DASD
___	7. disk tracks	g.	Winchester technology
___	8. block	h.	on-line
___	9. seek time	i.	ordered by key
___	10. track	j.	move access arm

Fill-In

1. Name the two most common media for secondary storage.

   1.a. ____________________

   b. ____________________

2. What is a technique for processing transactions in any order they occur?

   2. ____________________

3. List three benefits of secondary storage:

   3.a. ____________________

   b. ____________________

   c. ____________________

4. What is the name of the chip that acts as a disk drive?

   4. ____________________

5. What is the communication said to be when the user maintains a dialogue with the computer? 5. ______

6. What is the name for the electromagnet that can read magnetized areas on tape and convert them into electrical impulses? 6. ______

7. Name the two reels that are used with magnetic tape. 7.a. ______

b. ______

8. Optical storage technology is categorized according to what type of ability? 8. ______

9. What does CD-ROM stand for? 9. ______

10. What are two terms for the stopping space between records? 10.a. ______

b. ______

11. What process is used to avoid wasting space on a tape? 11. ______

12. What is the primary advantage of optical disk technology? 12. ______

13. Name the three kinds of components in a sealed data module. 13.a. ______

b. ______

c. ______

14. List the four primary factors that determine the time needed to access disk data. **14.a.** ______________________

b. ______________________

c. ______________________

d. ______________________

15. What are three major methods of organization for storing files of data in secondary storage? **15.a.** ______________________

b. ______________________

c. ______________________

16. What does sequential batch processing require before transactions can be used to update a file? **16.** ______________________

17. What is a unique identifier for a record called? **17.** ______________________

18. The smallest unit of raw data is: **18.** ______________________

19. Organizing data vertically on disk is called what method? **19.** ______________________

20. The two terms for the process used in direct file processing to get the numerical representation of a record's address are **20.a.** ______________________

b. ______________________

Test Answers

Multiple Choice

1. d	6. b	11. d	16. c	21. d
2. c	7. d	12. c	17. c	22. c
3. d	8. b	13. b	18. b	23. a
4. a	9. a	14. b	19. a	24. d
5. c	10. c	15. a	20. d	25. d

True/False

1. T	6. T	11. T	16. F	21. F
2. T	7. F	12. T	17. F	22. F
3. F	8. T	13. T	18. F	23. F
4. F	9. F	14. F	19. T	24. T
5. T	10. F	15. T	20. F	25. T

Matching

1. h	6. b
2. c	7. a
3. f	8. e
4. g	9. j
5. i	10. d

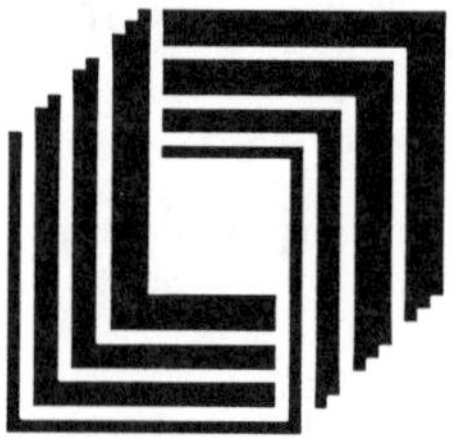

YOUR PHOTOS ON A CD

For an extra fee, about a dollar per frame, you can have the vacation shots of the kids at the seashore stored on a compact disk that can be viewed on your TV using a special CD player. Kodak, the first one to the marketplace with this innovation, is betting that shutterbugs will soon be buying the machines, to nestle alongside their TVs and VCRs. Meanwhile, adventuresome folks can pull the photos from the disks right into their home computers and manipulate the images, placing the baby afloat on a fluffy cloud or, perhaps, transmuting Aunt Martha's head onto the body of the family cat.

Fill-In

1.a. magnetic tape
 b. magnetic disk

2. transaction processing

3.a. economy
 b. reliability
 c. convenience

4. RAM disk

5. interactive

6. read/write head

7.a. supply reel
 b. take-up reel

8. read-write

9. compact disk read-only memory

10.a. interrecord gap (IRG)
 b. interblock gap (IBG)

11. blocking

12. high capacity

13.a. disks
 b. access arms
 c. read/write heads

14.a. seek time
 b. head switching
 c. rotational delay
 d. data transfer

15.a. sequential file
 b. direct file
 c. indexed file

16. sorted

17. key

18. character

19. cylinder method

20.a. hashing
 b. randomizing

Close to Home

Although you will probably not encounter full-size magnetic tapes and disk packs in your immediate environment, but it is quite likely that you will be using storage media for small computers directly in your school, home, or office. Be sure that you pay attention to the instructions for care that are listed on diskettes; the most important is that you keep the diskettes protected. If you have so many files on hard disk that backing them up on diskettes is tedious, consider a tape backup system.

CHAPTER

5

Communications: Linking Computers Worldwide

Learning Objectives

- ❑ Introduction to the evolution of data communications systems, from centralized data processing systems, to teleprocessing systems, to distributed data processing, to local area networks.
- ❑ Knowledge of data transmissions methods, including types of signals, modulation, and choices among transmission modes.
- ❑ Differentiating the different kinds of communication links.
- ❑ Acquaintance with the role of carriers and regulation.
- ❑ Understanding network configurations.
- ❑ Acquaintance with examples of networking such as electronic mail, voice mail, teleconferencing, facsimilie technology, electronic fund transfers, electronic data interchange, commercial communications services, workgroup computing, bulletin boards, shopping, and computer commuting.

Why This Chapter Is Important

If it seems as if the whole world is wired together into one gigantic computer network, this is not too far from the truth. Whatever the reality, it is certainly technologically possible to do just that. Thus it becomes important to have some understanding of the underlying concepts that support networking.

Chapter Outline

ON-LINE VACATION

New York to London for $150? Maybe. In the world of electronic globe-trotting, computer users can hook up on-line and search for bargain travel services.

To set yourself up, you need a personal computer, a modem, special software, and the phone number, user number, and password provided by the service (such as Prodigy or CompuServe).

Key Words

Acoustic coupler ______________________________

Amplitude modulation ______________________________

Analog transmission ______________________________

Asynchronous transmission ______________________________

Auto-answer ______________________________

Auto-dial ______________________________

Auto-disconnect ______________________________

Automatic redial ______________________________

Bandwidth ______________________________

Bridge ______________________________

Brouter ______________________________

Bulletin board systems (BBS) ______________________________

Bus network ______________________________

Cable interface unit ______________________________

Carrier wave ______________________________

Carterfone decision ______________________________

Centralized data processing ______________________________

Client/server network ______________________________

Coaxial cables ______________________________

Collaborative software ______________________________

JUST THE FAX, MA'AM

How would you like you fingerprints taken and identified right there by the side of the road? The FBI has an interesting on-site identification system in mind. The key is high tech equipment, including a fax machine, right in the patrol car. A prototype system uses a scanning machine to collect a person's fingerprints and send the data via local police stations to the FBI's central computer in Washington, D. C. There the fingerprints are compared with those on file for 320,000 wanted criminals. If a match is found, a picture of the person is returned by fax to confirm identification. The entire procedure would takes less than a minute.

Common carrier ______________________

CompuServe ______________________

Computer conferencing ______________________

Data communications system ______________________

Demodulation ______________________

Digital transmission ______________________

Direct-connect modem ______________________

Distributed data processing (DDP) ______________________

Electronic funds transfer (EFT) ______________________

Electronic mail ______________________

Ethernet ______________________

External modem ____________________

Facsimile technology (fax) ____________________

Fax board ____________________

Federal Communication Commission ____________________

Fiber optics ____________________

Frequency modulation ____________________

Front-end processor ____________________

Full-duplex transmission ____________________

Gateway ____________________

Groupware ____________________

Half-duplex transmission ____________________

TOYS BY NETWORK

Suppose you had 497 toy stores scattered across the United States, another 126 sprinkled among international locales - and they needed to communicate with each other. A computer network system seems the obvious answer, and Toys R Us, Inc. has done exactly that.

The company uses a mainframe to manage the network and process information coming in from the field. The system coordinates orders from stores to distribution centers, analyzes store data to forecast marketing trends, and helps distribute information to stores. Definitely not child's play.

Hayes compatible

Host computer

Information utility

Integrated services digital network

Internal modem

Internet

Leased lines

Link

Local area network (LAN)

Metropolitan area network (MAN)

Micro-to-mainframe link

Microwave transmission

Modem

Modulation

Multipoint line

Network

Network cable

Node

Noise

Open Systems Interconnection (OSI)

Packet switching

Peer-to-peer network

Phase modulation ____________________
____
____

Point-to-point line ____________________
____
____

Private line ____________________
____
____

Prodigy ____________________
____
____

Protocol ____________________
____
____

Repeater ____________________
____
____

Ring network ____________________
____
____

Router ____________________
____
____

Satellite transmission ____________________
____
____

Server ____________________
____
____

Simplex transmission ____________________
____
____

Star network ____________________
____
____

Start/stop transmission ____________________
____
____

Switched line systems ____________________
____
____

Synchronous transmission ____________________
____
____

Systems Network Architecture (SNA)
____
____

Tariff ____________________
____
____

Telecommunications ____________________
____
____

Telecommuting ____________________
____
____

Teleconferencing ____________________
____
____

Teleprocessing ____________________
____
____

Terminal emulation software ____________________
____
____

Time-delay ____________________

Token passing ____________________

Topology ____________________

Transponder ____________________

Value added network (VAN) ____________________

Videoconferencing ____________________

Videotex ____________________

Voice mail ____________________

Wide Area Network (WAN) ____________________

Wire pair ____________________

Workstation ____________________

Study Hints

This is one of those chapters with lots of new terminology; fortunately, much of it is self-descriptive. However, before you take the trouble to learn all these terms, you might ask your instructor just how much detail is required; some instructors may prefer that you just get the big picture.

CURLING UP WITH A GOOD COMPUTER

Would you like to select a book from a menu on your computer monitor, and then have the words zapped to you instantly on the screen? If so, consider the Paperless Readers Club, sponsored by a Florida company called Booklink. From an environmental viewpoint, paper is saved. Furthermore, a book will never be "out of print."

Self-Test

Multiple Choice

1. Data communications systems are
   a. totally centralized
   b. computer systems
   c. telephone companies
   d. outdated

2. Centralized processing with the flexibility of time-sharing is known as
   a. a teleprocessing system
   b. DDP
   c. a ring network
   d. telecommuting

3. Computer systems that use data communications equipment to connect two or more computers and their resources are
   a. host computer systems
   b. teleprocessing systems
   c. networks
   d. centralized

4. When all hardware, software, storage, and processing is housed in one location it is called
   a. a time-sharing system
   b. a DDP system
   c. centralized processing
   d. a host computer system

5. Transmission permitting data to move only one way at a time is
   a. half-duplex
   b. full-duplex
   c. simplex
   d. start/stop

6. The process of converting from analog to digital is called
   a. modulation
   b. telecommuting
   c. line switching
   d. demodulation

7. The device used with satellite transmission that ensures that strong outgoing signals do not interfere with weak incoming signals is called a
   a. microwave
   b. coupler
   c. transponder
   d. modem

8. The most convenient communication links are
   a. coaxial cables
   b. telephone lines
   c. via satellites
   d. via microwaves

9. IBM's Token Ring Network controls access to the network using
   a. facsimile
   b. auto-disconnect
   c. a bus
   d. token passing

10. Organizations approved to offer communications services are called
   a. AT&T networks
   b. value-added carriers
   c. star networks
   d. common carriers

11. A computer-based system in which a telephoned message is recorded in digital form and then forwarded to others is
   a. teleconferencing
   b. a bulletin board system
   c. voice mail
   d. telecommuting

12. One or more computers connected to a host computer is a
   a. ring network
   b. multistar network
   c. value-added network
   d. star network

13. Another name for a bridge is
   a. satellite
   b. router
   c. gateway
   d. common carrier

14. The physical layout of a LAN is called
   a. topology
   b. link
   c. contention
   d. telecommunications

15. A computer that relieves the central computer of some of the communication tasks is a
   a. communication link
   b. modem
   c. front-end processor
   d. resource computer

16. The type of modulation that changes the height of the signal is called
   a. frequency
   b. amplitude
   c. phase
   d. pre-phase

17. A network that assigns a portion of the network management to each node is called
   a. star
   b. switched
   c. ring
   d. bus

18. The signals produced by a computer or terminal to be sent over phone lines must be converted to
   a. modems
   b. digital signals
   c. analog signals
   d. microwaves

19. Each computer in a LAN is called a
   a. bus
   b. host
   c. node
   d. server

20. Microwave transmission, coaxial cables, and fiber optics are examples of
a. modems
b. communication links
c. common carriers
d. value-added networks

21. A network of geographically distant computers and terminals is called a
a. bus
b. brouter
c. WAN
d. LAN

22. Two LANs of the same type can be connected by a
a. bridge
b. bus
c. node
d. server

23. Graphics and other paperwork can being transmitted directly using what technology
a. videotex
b. facsimile
c. token passing
d. bulletin board

24. Home shopping via a computer network is called
a. gateway
b. videotex
c. EFT
d. teleconferencing

25. To make a personal computer act like a terminal, this type of software must be used
a. videotex
b. router
c. videoconferencing
d. terminal emulation

True/False

T F 1. Frequency modulation varies the position in time of a complete wave cycle.

T F 2. Local area networks are designed to share data and resources among several computers in the same geographical location.

T F 3. Terminals connected to a central computer via communication lines comprise a centralized data processing system.

T F 4. An auto-disconnect modem disconnects a call automatically when the other party hangs up or a disconnect message is received.

T F 5. Teleprocessing allows a user to make queries of a computer one thousand miles away.

T F 6. An internal modem is normally used with a variety of computers.

T F 7. A modem can be used for either modulation or demodulation.

T F 8. Start/stop transmission transmits characters in a stream.

T F 9. Satellites use line-of-sight transmission.

T F 10. Full-duplex allows transmission in both directions at once.

T F 11. Fiber optics are a cheaper form of communication wire cables.

T F 12. CCITT has endorsed the SNA communications protocol model.

T F 13. A multipoint configuration uses direct lines between terminal and the central computer.

T F 14. The majority of LANs use a ring structure.

T F 15. Synchronous transmission is also called start/stop transmission.

T F 16. Interactions among computer system components must a line protocol.

T F 17. A common carrier is an organization that has tariff to the FCC and been approved.

T F 18. Fax and videotex are identical technologies.

T F 19. A ring network has no central host computer.

T F 20. EFTs are one of many ways of communicating via computer networking.

T F 21. A gateway connects two similar computers.

T F 22. A bus network topology uses a central computer the server.

T F 23. Fax boards can be inserted into computers.

T F 24. Ethernet is a local area network system.

T F 25. Telecommuting is a form of information utility.

Matching I

___	1. modulation	a.	start/stop
___	2. fiber optics	b.	signal distortion
___	3. asynchronous	c.	remote processing
___	4. common carriers	d.	analog to digital
___	5. demodulation	e.	remote access
___	6. DDP	f.	communication link
___	7. modem compatibility	g.	digital to analog
___	8. ring network	h.	Hayes compatibility
___	9. teleprocessing	i.	no central host computer
___	10. noise	j.	approved organizations

Matching II

___	1. e-mail	a.	home shopping
___	2. EFT	b.	twisted pairs
___	3. videotex	c.	direct connection
___	4. private lines	d.	send messages
___	5. tariff	e.	LAN layout
___	6. public network	f.	transfer money
___	7. topology	g.	leased lines
___	8. upload	h.	Internet
___	9. wire pairs	i.	service rates
___	10. point-to-point	j.	retrieve and store files

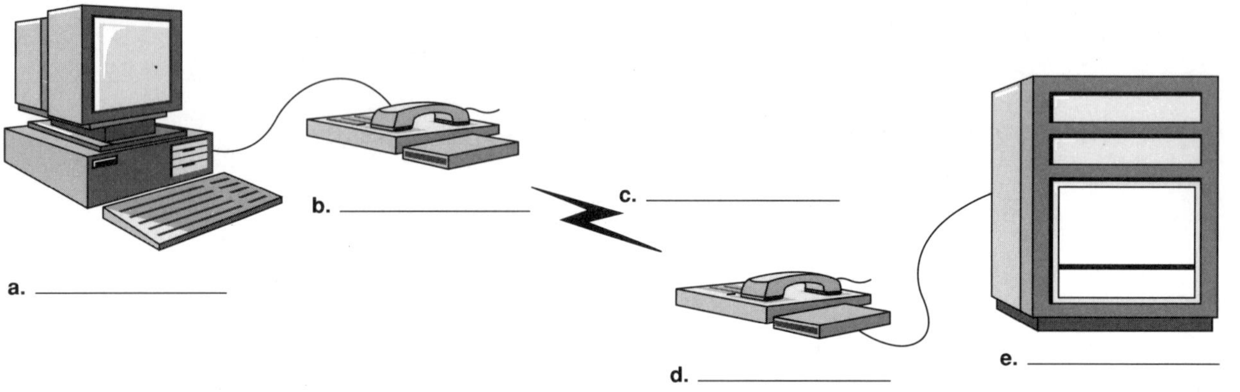

Figure 1 Communications system components.

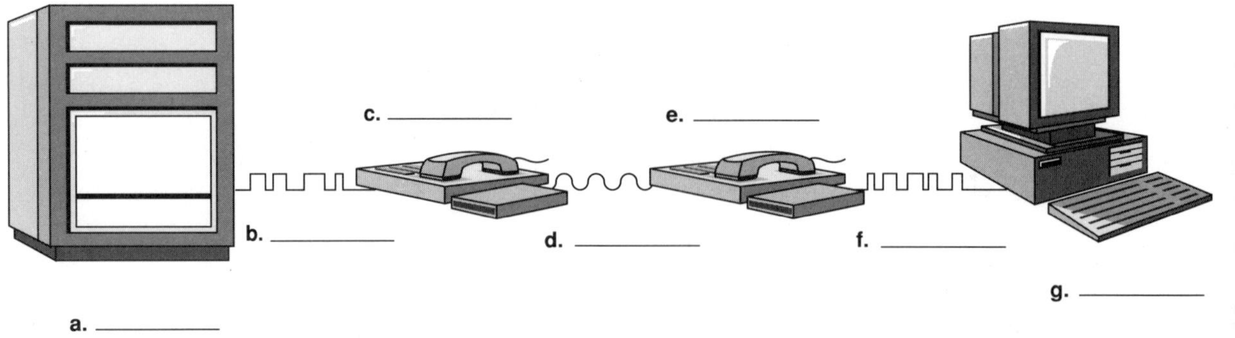

Figure 2 Modems and signals.

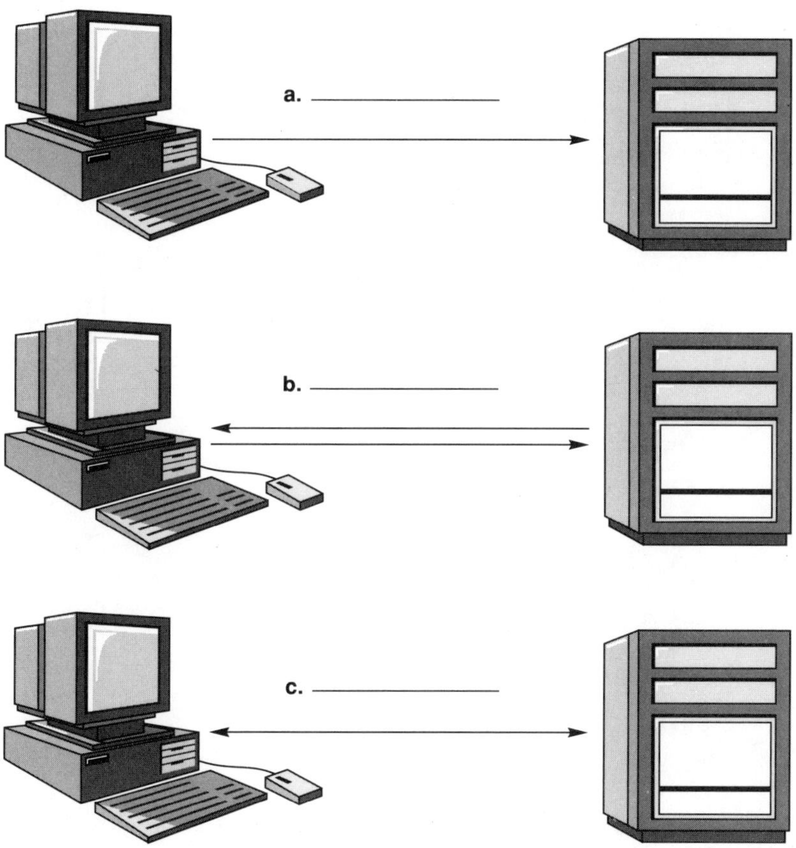

Figure 3 Transmission directions.

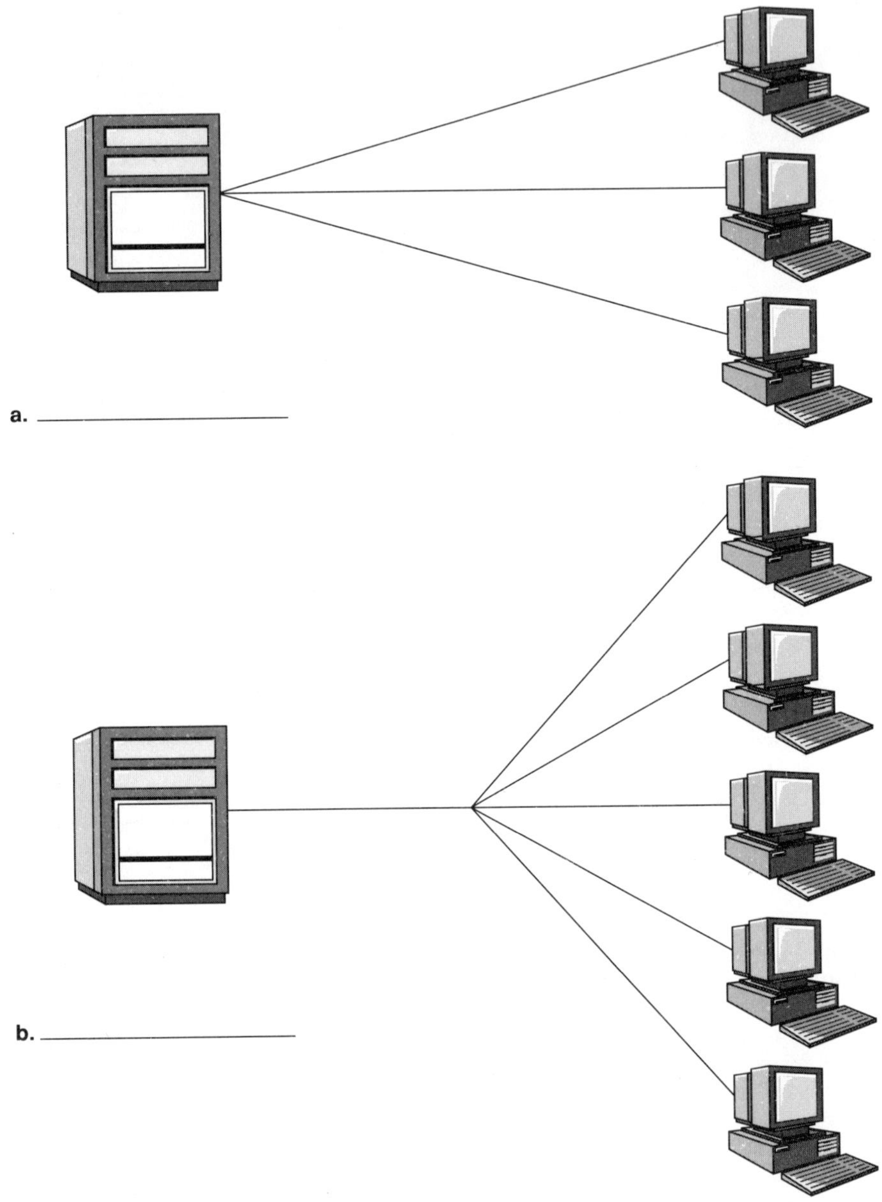

Figure 4 Point-to-point and multipoint lines.

Fill-In

1. What is the term for computer systems that transmit data over telephone lines? 1. ______________
2. What does OSI stand for? 2. ______________
3. Which kind of signal do most telephone lines require? 3. ______________
4. What device converts a digital signal to an analog signal or vice versa? 4. ______________
5. What are Prodigy and CompuServe examples of? 5. ______________
6. What type of modem allows a telephone receiver to be connected to a portable computer? 6. ______________
7. What is the name of IBM's standard protocol? 7. ______________
8. What is the general term for the use of technology in the office 8. ______________
9. What kind of computer relieves the central computer of some communication tasks? 9. ______________
10. What kind of network links distant computers and terminals? 10. ______________
11. What principal type of line configuration describes a direct connection between each terminal and the central computer? 11. ______________
12. What must an organization wishing to offer communications services submit to the FCC? 12. ______________
13. How does IBM's Token Ring Network control access to the cable? 13. ______________

14. Identify the two types of lines offered by common carriers. 14.a. ____________ b. ____________

15. What does the acronym VAN stand for? 15. ____________

16. What is the term for computer networks that share resources in a limited geographical location? 16. ____________

17. What is a video display catalog used to shop at home called? 17. ____________

18. What form of retailing allows consumers to order items through computer terminals? 18. ____________

19. In addition to auto-answer and auto-disconnect, list three typical modem features. 19.a. ____________ b. ____________ c. ____________

20. What does BBS stand for? 20. ____________

21. What hardware device connects two dissimilar networks? 21. ____________

22. The most popular type of LAN: 22. ____________

23. To communicate with a larger computer, a personal computer must use what kind of software? 23. ____________

24. IBM's protocol is called: 24. ____________

25. The court decision that permits other communication companies to use the telephone network: 25. ____________

Test Answers

Multiple Choice

1. b	6. d	11. c	16. b	21. c
2. a	7. c	12. d	17. d	22. a
3. c	8. b	13. b	18. c	23. b
4. c	9. d	14. a	19. c	24. b
5. a	10. d	15. c	20. b	25. d

True/False

1. F	6. F	11. T	16. T	21. F
2. T	7. T	12. F	17. T	22. F
3. F	8. F	13. F	18. F	23. T
4. T	9. F	14. F	19. T	24. T
5. T	10. T	15. F	20. T	25. F

Matching I

1. g	6. c
2. f	7. h
3. a	8. i
4. j	9. e
5. d	10. b

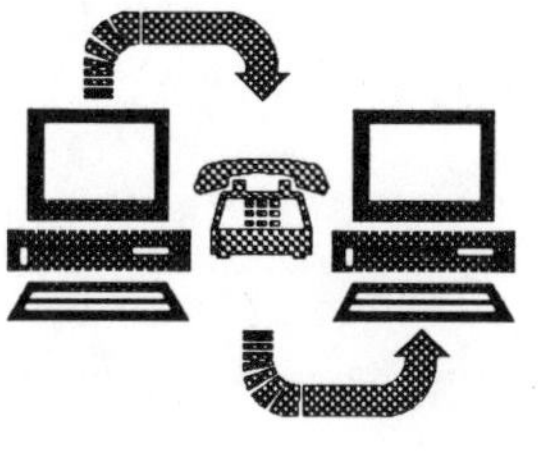

Matching II

1. d	6. h
2. f	7. e
3. a	8. j
4. g	9. b
5. i	10. c

Figures

Figure 1
a. sending device
b. modem
c. communications link
d. modem
e. central processing unit

Figure 2
a. central processing unit
b. digital signal
c. modem
d. analog signal
e. modem
f. digital signal
g. terminal

Figure 3
a. simplex
b. half-duplex
c. full-duplex

Figure 4
a. point-to-point
b. multipoint

Fill-In

1. data communications systems
2. open systems interconnection
3. analog
4. a modem
5. information utilities
6. an acoustic coupler
7. systems network architecture
8. office automation
9. front-end processor
10. wide area network
11. point-to-point line
12. a tariff
13. token passing

14.a. private
b. switched

15. value-added network
16. bulletin board systems
17. videotex
18. telecommunications

19.a. auto-dial
b. automatic redial
c. time-delay

20. bulletin board systems
21. gateway
22. Ethernet
23. terminal emulation software
24. Systems Network Architecture
25. Carterfone

Close to Home

Have you given any thought to what you might do with your own personal computer access to networks? The list of possibilities in the main text is extensive, but you may find that you have other ideas. In many parts of the country, something akin to the CB radio craze seems to be developing, complete with "handles," that is, individual colorful names such as Big Red and Starshine. Rules of courtesy are already established: It is not considered polite, for instance, to eavesdrop on the communications of others without identifying yourself by your handle. So - send electronic mail, learn a language, and do your shopping, all with the aid of networks. And make new friends.

CHAPTER

6

Programming and Languages

Learning Objectives

- ❑ Understanding what programmers do and do not do.
- ❑ Introduction to how programmers define a problem, plan the solution, and then code, test, and document the program.
- ❑ Introduction to the levels of programming languages - machine, assembly, high level, very high level, and natural.
- ❑ Introduction to some important programming languages.
- ❑ Introduction to the concept of object-oriented languages.

Why This Chapter Is Important

For many computer professionals, programming is what computers are all about.

In addition, although this chapter makes no attempt to be comprehensive, it gives you some feeling for the development of levels of languages. If you have career plans in the direction of programming, this chapter provides some insights to how languages are used and highlights some of the languages you are likely to use in your career.

Most people, however, although touched markedly by the computer revolution, will not actually learn to program. If you expect to stay on the periphery of the computer field, then you can at least gain some insight into how programmers work.

Chapter Outline

Why Programming?

What Programmers Do

The Programming Process
1. Defining the Problem
2. Planning the Solution
3. Coding the Program
4. Testing the Program
5. Documenting the Program

Programming Languages

Levels of Language
- Machine Language
- Assembly Languages
- High-Level Languages
- Very High-Level Languages
- Natural Languages

Choosing a Language

FORTRAN: The First High-Level Language

COBOL: The Language of Business

BASIC: For Beginners and Others

Pascal: The Language of Simplicity

Ada: The Language of Standardization?

C: A Portable Language

Some Other Languages

Object-Oriented Programming

Some Advice

Is Programming for You?

WRITING GAME SOFTWARE? USE MACHINE LANGUAGE!

To write good computer games, you need a thorough understanding of the inner workings of the computer. Furthermore, games are almost always written in a machine language to ensure maximum speed.

To write game software, you need an original idea. In fact, if your game looks too much like an existing game, you can expect a lawsuit. You also need a machine with high-resolution multicolor graphics, sound, and joystick input capability. An excellent get-started book is *Apple Graphics and Arcade Design* by Jeffrey Stanton, The Book Company, 11223 South Hindry Ave., Los Angeles, CA 90045.

Key Words

APL ______________________________
____
____

Artificial intelligence ______________
____
____

Assembler ______________________
____
____

Assembly program ______________
____
____

BASIC ______________________
____
____

C ______________________________
____
____

COBOL ______________________
____
____

Compiler ______________________
____
____

Debugging ______________________
____
____

Desk-checking ______________________
____
____

Diagnostics ______________________
____
____

Documentation ______________________
____
____

Expert system ______________________
____
____

Flowchart ______________________
____
____

FORTH ______________________
____
____

Fourth-generation language ________
____
____

FORTRAN ______________________
____
____

Interpreter ______________________
____
____

Link/load phase ______________
____
____

Load module ______________________
____
____

Logic error ______________________
____
____

LOGO ______________________
____
____

Modula-2 ______________________
____
____

Nonprocedural language ______________________
____
____

Object module ______________________
____
____

PILOT ______________________
____
____

PL/I ______________________
____
____

Procedural language ______________________
____
____

PROLOG ______________________
____
____

Pseudocode ______________________
____
____

RPG ______________________
____
____

Smalltalk ______________________
____
____

Structure chart ______________________
____
____

Structured programming ______________________
____
____

Syntax error ______________________
____
____

Translator ______________________
____
____

Turbo Pascal ______________________
____
____

Visual programming languages ______________________
____
____

Study Hints

The material in this chapter may be seem a bit esoteric if you have no experience or interest in programming. However, you can understand what programmers do, in a general way, by reviewing the material. If you need to know the ins and outs of the languages, then the extensive tests in this chapter should help.

Self-Test

Multiple Choice

1. Programmers spend relatively little time working with
   a. software
   b. people
   c. hardware
   d. reports

2. In preparing a program, one should first
   a. plan the solution
   b. document the program
   c. code the program
   d. define the problem

3. During the development of a program, drawing a flowchart is a means to
   a. plan the solution
   b. define the problem
   c. code the program
   d. analyze the problem

4. An English-like language that one can use as a designing tool is
   a. BASIC
   b. PL/I
   c. pseudocode
   d. Pascal

5. In preparing a program, desk-checking and translating are examples of
   a. coding
   b. testing
   c. planning
   d. documenting

6. The process of detecting, locating, and correcting mistakes by running the program is called
   a. desk-checking
   b. debugging
   c. translating
   d. documenting

7. Comments in the program itself are called
   a. interpreters
   b. diagnostic messages
   c. translators
   d. documentation

8. A COBOL program has how many divisions
   a. four
   b. five
   c. two
   d. seven

9. The first high-level language to be introduced was
   a. COBOL
   b. Pascal
   c. FORTRAN
   d. Ada

10. BASIC was developed at
   a. Dartmouth
   b. MIT
   c. Yale
   d. Princeton

11. The language named for a French mathematician is
   a. C
   b. Pascal
   c. Ada
   d. Modula-2

12. Specifying the kind of input, processing, and output required for a program occurs when those involved are
   a. planning the solution
   b. coding the program
   c. flowcharting the problem
   d. defining the problem

13. Error messages provided by a compiler are called
   a. bugs
   b. translations
   c. diagnostics
   d. mistakes

14. After stating the solution to a problem in pseudocode, the next step in development would be
   a. testing the program
   b. documenting the program
   c. coding the program
   d. translating the program

15. The highest level languages are called
   a. 4GL
   b. self-documenting
   c. high-level
   d. natural

16. Entrepreneurs are using this language on their own personal computers to compete with established software firms
   a. C
   b. LOGO
   c. COBOL
   d. FORTRAN

17. A BASIC interpreter translates a program
   a. all at once
   b. into BASIC
   c. one line at a time
   d. like a compiler

18. Software that translates assembly language into machine language is
   a. a binary translator
   b. an assembler
   c. a compiler
   d. usually unnecessary

19. A standardized business language is
   a. CODASYL
   b. COBOL
   c. BASIC
   d. Ada

20. In developing a program, documentation should be done
   a. as the last step
   b. only to explain errors
   c. throughout the process
   d. only during the design phase

21. A language that is popular for natural language programming is
   a. PILOT
   b. PROLOG
   c. ALGOL
   d. LOGO

22. A language designed to generate routine business reports is
   a. COBOL
   b. RPG
   c. LISP
   d. ALGOL

23. The lowest level of programming language is
   a. nonprocedural language
   b. BASIC
   c. assembly language
   d. machine language

24. An assembly language uses
   a. English words
   b. 0s and 1s
   c. mnemonic codes
   d. binary digits

25. Smalltalk, a language that uses a mouse to direct movements on the CRT screen, is
   a. procedural oriented
   b. problem oriented
   c. nonprocedural
   d. object oriented

True/False

T F 1. To learn how to program, one must first understand the details of the hardware.

T F 2. Developing a program requires just two steps, coding and testing.

T F 3. A flowchart is an example of pseudocode.

T F 4. Desk-checking is the first phase of testing a program.

T F 5. A translator is a form of hardware that translates a program into language the computer can understand.

T F 6. A compiler translates an entire program at one time.

T F 7. Debugging is the process of locating program errors.

T F 8. FORWARD and LEFT are typical LOGO commands.

T F 9. Pseudocode can be used to plan and execute a program.

T F 10. 4GLs increase clarity but reduce productivity.

T F 11. PL/I was designed as a compromise for scientific and business uses.

T F 12. Pascal is particularly easy to use because it has fewer features than most languages.

T F 13. COBOL is divided into four parts called areas.

T F 14. BASIC is especially suited for large and complex programs.

T F 15. FORTRAN stands for FORms TRANsfer.

T F 16. Expressing a problem solution in Pascal is an example of coding a program.

T F 17. Diagnostic messages are concerned with improper use of the programming language.

T F 18. An assembler program translates high-level language into assembly language.

T F 19. The most common business language in use today is COBOL.

T F 20. PROLOG is used for artificial intelligence programming.

T F 21. COBOL is a relatively machine-independent language because it is a standardized language.

T F 22. Another name for a high-level language is 4GL.

T F 23. The highest-level languages are simply called high-level languages.

T F 24. FORTRAN is primarily used in scientific environments.

T F 25. Lower-level languages are closer to the language the computer itself uses than are higher-level languages.

Matching I

___	1. diagnostics	a. BASIC
___	2. coding	b. compiler output
___	3. debugging	c. desk-checking
___	4. object module	d. object oriented
___	5. RPG	e. planning the solution
___	6. pseudocode	f. syntax errors
___	7. 4GL	g. program listings
___	8. Turbo Pascal	h. reports
___	9. documentation	i. nonprocedural
___	10. proofreading	j. logic errors

Matching II

___	1. problem oriented	a. FORTRAN
___	2. assembly language	b. FORTH
___	3. 1st high-level language	c. user friendly
___	4. general purpose	d. LOGO
___	5. weapons systems	e. Smalltalk
___	6. nonprocedural	f. RPG
___	7. object oriented	g. Pascal
___	8. efficient memory	h. Ada
___	9. turtle	i. mnemonic codes
___	10. language of simplicity	j. PL/I

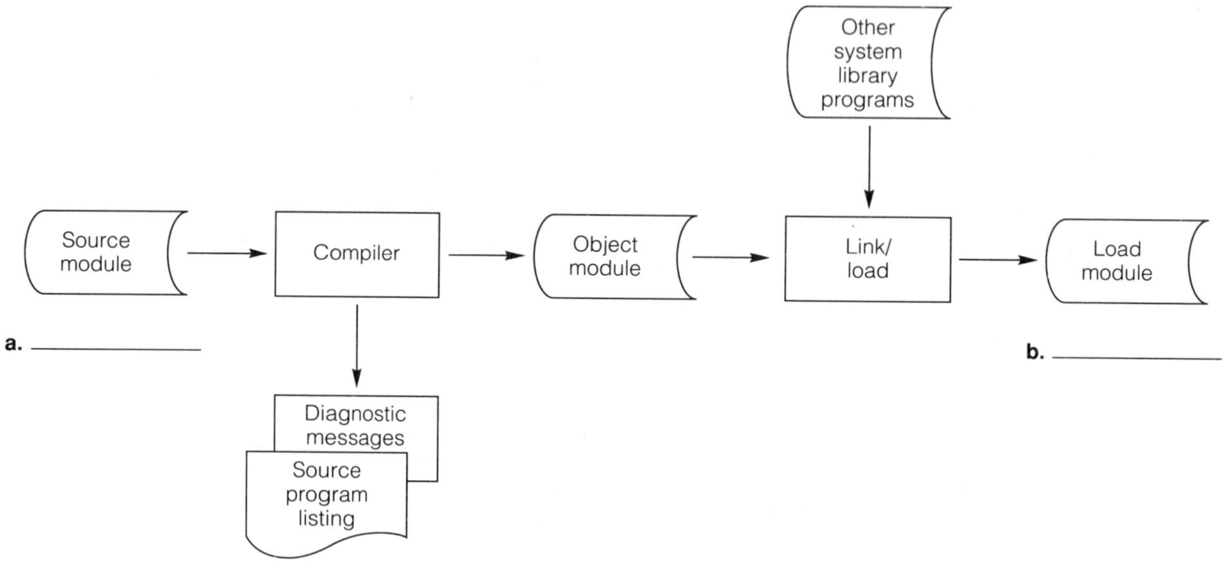

Figure 1 Preparing a program for execution

Fill-In

1. What is the use of a natural language to access a knowledge base called? 1. ____________

2. What is the term for languages that use abbreviations or mnemonic code to replace numbers? 2. ____________

3. Which language is used for real-time control tasks and is designed to be speedy and memory-efficient? 3. ____________

4. What level of language is FOCUS? 4. ____________

5. What is the name for a translator that translates high-level languages into machine language? **5.** ____________________

6. What term describes the fact that COBOL needs few ongoing comments in the program? **6.** ____________________

7. The two languages written by Niklaus Wirth: **7.a.** ____________________

b. ____________________

8. How many levels of language were described in the chapter? **8.** ____________________

9. Name a high-level language that is problem oriented. **9.** ____________________

10. Which language is specifically designed to write systems software? **10.** ____________________

11. List the divisions parts of a COBOL program. **11.a.** ____________________

b. ____________________

c. ____________________

d. ____________________

12. Which language is a dialect of LISP that is particularly suitable for children? **12.** ____________________

13. Name an object-oriented language. **13.** ____________________

14. Which language was sponsored by the Pentagon? **14.** ____________________

15. Name the language that is popular in computer science programs. 15. ____________

16. Which language was introduced in 1964 by IBM as a compromise between FORTRAN and COBOL? 16. ____________

17. What kind of language tells the computer what needs to be done, as opposed to how? 17. ____________

18. What are languages that resemble spoken languages called? 18. ____________

19. Which high-level language is scientifically oriented? 19. ____________

20. List four benefits of 4GLs. 20.a. ____________

b. ____________

c. ____________

d. ____________

21. Which of the five steps of the programming process is best done throughout the process? 21. ____________

22. What are two common methods of planning the solution to a problem? 22.a. ____________

b. ____________

23. List the three phases of testing a program. 23.a. ____________

b. ____________

c. ____________

24. What are you doing when you express a program in COBOL or BASIC? 24. ____________

25. What is the term for the error messages that a translator provides?

25. ____________________

Test Answers

Multiple Choice

1. c	6. b	11. b	16. a	21. b
2. d	7. d	12. d	17. c	22. b
3. a	8. a	13. c	18. b	23. d
4. c	9. c	14. c	19. b	24. c
5. b	10. a	15. d	20. c	25. d

True/False

1. F	6. T	11. T	16. T	21. T
2. F	7. T	12. T	17. T	22. F
3. F	8. T	13. F	18. F	23. F
4. T	9. F	14. F	19. T	24. T
5. F	10. F	15. F	20. T	25. T

Matching I

1. f	6. e
2. a	7. i
3. j	8. d
4. b	9. g
5. h	10. c

Matching II

1. f	6. c
2. i	7. e
3. a	8. b
4. j	9. d
5. h	10. g

Figure

Figure 1
a. original program
b. executable program

Fill-In

1. knowledge-based system
2. assembly language
3. FORTH
4. very high-level language
5. compiler
6. self-documenting
7. a. Pascal
   b. Modula-2
8. five
9. RPG
10. Modula-2
11. a. identification division
    b. environment division
    c. data division
    d. procedure division
12. LOGO
13. Smalltalk, Turbo Pascal, or C++
14. Ada
15. Pascal
16. PL/I
17. nonprocedural
18. natural language
19. FORTRAN
20. a. results oriented
    b. improved productivity
    c. programmers / nonprogrammers
    d. shield users from hardware, logic
21. documentation
22. a. flowcharting
    b. writing pseudocode
23. a. desk-checking
    b. translating
    c. debugging
24. coding
25. diagnostics

Close to Home

If you are contemplating a career as a computer programmer, this chapter is, of course, of vital interest to you. From this foundation you can move on to the use of a programming language and actually plan and develop computer programs.

If you plan to write programs on your home computer, the most common language by far, and the easiest, is BASIC. However, some major languages mentioned in the chapter are available for personal computers, particularly Pascal and C.

CHAPTER

7

Operating Systems: The Hidden Software

Learning Objectives

- ❑ Appreciating the need for operating systems.
- ❑ Understanding the benefits of multiprogramming and time-sharing.
- ❑ Understanding the special problems related to sharing resources.
- ❑ Knowledge of translators and service programs.
- ❑ Introduction to generic operating systems.
- ❑ Introduction to operating systems for personal computers.

Why This Chapter Is Important

The operating system is the connection between you and the computer. In any system you may use, you will have to be aware of the use of the operating system and the underlying concepts.

Chapter Outline

Managing Shared Resources: The Traffic Cop
- Resource Allocation
- Memory Management
  - Foreground and Background
  - Virtual Storage
  - Memory Protection
- Spooling

Service Programs

UNIX and Generic Operating Systems
- The UNIX Graduates
- Is UNIX a Standard?

Operating Systems for Personal Computers

Using MS-DOS
- DOS Commands
- DOS and Disk Drives
  - Disk Drive Configurations
  - The Default Drive
  - Diskette Functions

Operating Environments: The User Interface
- The Command-Line Interface
- Shells
- The Graphical User Interface
- The Gesture-Based Interface

Do I Really Need to Know All This?

Key Words

Background ______________________

Booting ______________________

Command-line interface ______________________

Current drive ______________________

Deadlock ______________________________
____
____

Event driven ______________________________
____
____

External DOS commands ______________
____
____

Foreground ______________________________
____
____

Gesture-based interface ______________
____
____

Graphical user interface (GUI) ________
____
____

Internal DOS commands ______________
____
____

Interrupt ______________________________
____
____

Memory management ________________
____
____

Memory protection __________________
____
____

Multiprogramming __________________
____
____

Multitasking ______________________________
____
____

Operating environment ______________
____
____

Operating system __________________
____
____

Page ______________________________
____
____

Page frame ______________________________
____
____

Parallel processing __________________
____
____

Prompt ______________________________
____
____

Real storage ______________________________
____
____

Resource allocation ________________
____
____

Response time ______________________
____
____

Round-robin scheduling ______________
____
____

Shell ______________________________

Spooling program ______________________________

Supervisor program ______________________________

Time-sharing ______________________________

Time slice ______________________________

Utility program ______________________________

UNIX ______________________________

Virtual memory ______________________________

Virtual storage ______________________________

Study Hints

The information in this chapter is serious and rather technical. Your best bet for gaining a true understanding of operating systems is to apply the principles presented here to the operating system in your own computer environment.

Self-Test

Multiple Choice

1. An operating system is a
   a. set of users
   b. set of programs
   c. form of time-sharing
   d. supervisor program

2. In multiprogramming, two or more programs can be executed
   a. by optimizing compilers
   b. at the same time
   c. with two computers
   d. concurrently

3. Time-sharing of resources by users is usually
   a. based on time slices c. based on input
   b. event driven d. operated by spooling

4. Management of an operating system is handled by
   a. an interpreter c. the supervisor program
   b. utility programs d. the CPU

5. The process of allocating main memory to programs and keeping the programs in memory separate from each other is called
   a. memory protection c. memory management
   b. virtual storage d. real storage

6. Unix is an example of a(n)
   a. assembler c. generic operating system
   b. source module d. utility program

7. The technique in shared systems that avoids interspersed printout from several programs is
   a. paging c. queuing
   b. segmentation d. spooling

8. The technique whereby part of the program is stored on disk and is brought into memory for execution as needed is called
   a. memory allocation c. real storage
   b. virtual storage d. prioritized memory

9. A user interface that requires remembering commands:
   a. UNIX c. CLI
   b. gesture d. GUI

10. Which is NOT a typical use of diskettes:
   a. virtual storage c. backup
   b. program installation d. data

11. Another name for an operating environment is
   a. window c. layer
   b. shell d. supervisor

12. Loading the operating system into a personal computer is called
   a. booting c. prompting
   b. linking d. paging

13. Which is a graphical shell?
a. UNIX
b. utility program
c. page
d. GUI

14. In multiprogramming, the process of confining each program to certain defined limits in memory is called
a. spooling
b. program scheduling
c. virtual storage
d. memory protection

15. The corresponding memory spaces for pages are called
a. segments
b. page block
c. page frames
d. page modules

16. The generic operating system developed by Bell Labs is
a. CP/M
b. TRS-DOS
c. UNIX
d. MS-DOS

17. Operating system overlay:
a. page
b. shell
c. page frame
d. virtual memory

18. Take-a-turn time-sharing:
a. spooling
b. round-robin
c. interfacing
d. prompting

19. Page frames are typically
a. 1K or 2K bytes
b. 2K or 3K bytes
c. 3K or 4K bytes
d. 2K or 4K bytes

20. Another name for multiprogramming:
a. framing
b. booting
c. multitasking
d. spooling

21. Programs waiting to be run are kept on the disk in
a. page frames
b. shells
c. the background
d. queues

22. Prewritten standard file-handling programs are called
a. assemblers
b. supervisors
c. modules
d. utilities

23. DOS programs that reside on the disk are called
a. external
b. generic
c. default
d. internal

24. Another name for virtual memory is
a. virtual storage
b. background
c. source program
d. object module

25. Which is NOT a user interface?
a. GUI
b. UNIX
c. gesture
d. CLI

True/False

T F 1. An operating system allocates resources with minimal operator intervention.

T F 2. The most important program in an operating system is the supervisor program.

T F 3. Multiprogramming means that two or more programs can run simultaneously.

T F 4. Time-sharing is effective because input/output speeds are so much faster than CPU speeds.

T F 5. The personal computer operating system standard was determined by Apple Computer.

T F 6. Background programs are usually batch programs.

T F 7. Virtual storage is a technique of memory management that appears to provide users with more memory space than is actually the case.

T F 8. With the virtual storage technique, secondary storage is considered real storage.

T F 9. One form of memory management is virtual storage.

T F 10. A gesture-based user interface uses a touch-sensitive screen.

T F 11. Spooling is a process that results in interspersed printout from several programs.

T F 12. Shell is another name for page.

T F 13. Applications programmers work directly with the operating system programs.

T F 14. Utility programs perform file conversions and sort/merge operations to avoid duplication of effort.

T F 15. In a given memory system, all page frames are the same size.

T F 16. CLI is easier to use than GUI.

T F 17. External DOS commands can be accessed the same way as internal DOS commands.

T F 18. Unix is a generic operating system that is run on mainframes, minicomputers, and microcomputers.

T F 19. In a multiprogramming environment, programs share computer resources.

T F 20. Windows is a popular graphical user interface.

T F 21. Another name for interrupt is deadlock.

T F 22. An interrupt is usually caused by system failure.

T F 23. Response time is the time it takes a program to run.

T F 24. Round-robin scheduling gives each user the processor in turn.

T F 25. Parallel processing permits simultaneous processing.

Matching I

___	1. memory management	a.	file handling
___	2. MS-DOS	b.	fixed memory spaces
___	3. user interface	c.	time slice
___	4. utility programs	d.	IBM PC
___	5. UNIX	e.	virtual storage
___	6. interrupt	f.	event driven
___	7. multiprogramming	g.	real storage
___	8. page frames	h.	CLI
___	9. time-sharing	i.	generic operating system
___	10. memory	j.	halt in processing

Matching II

___	1. deadlock	a.	current
___	2. parallel processing	b.	Windows
___	3. boot	c.	simultaneous
___	4. default	d.	signal the user
___	5. shell	e.	resource conflict
___	6. prompt	f.	gesture-based interface
___	7. multiprogramming	g.	in real storage
___	8. pen	h.	load the operating system
___	9. GUI	i.	multitasking
___	10. page frame	j.	operating environment

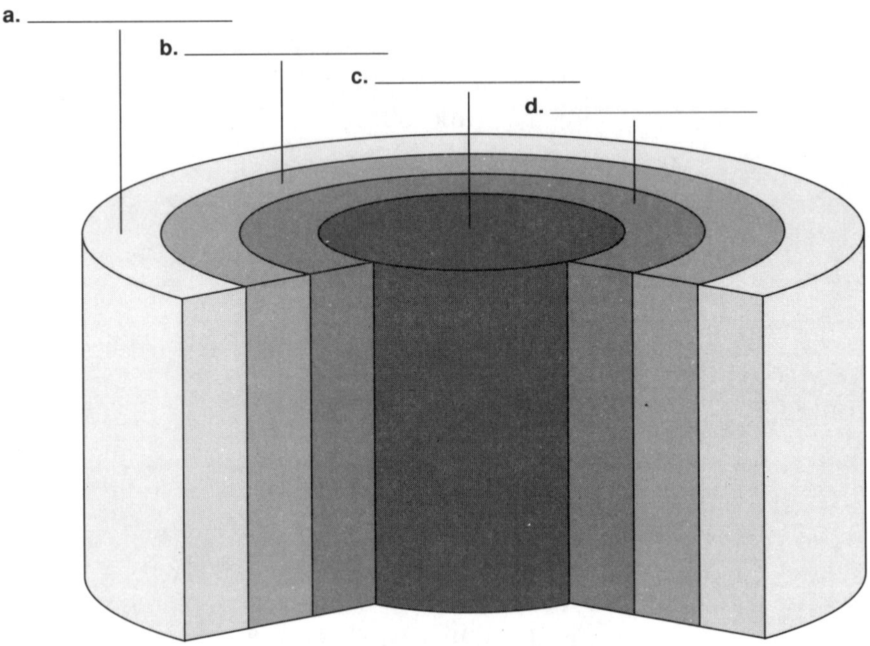

Figure 1 A conceptual diagram of an operating system.

Fill-In

1. List the three main functions of an operating system. **1.a.** ____________

   b. ____________

   c. ____________

2. What program remains for the most part in main memory and controls the entire operating system? **2.** ____________

3. What term is used for the time required between a user's request at the terminal and the computer's reply? **3.** ____________

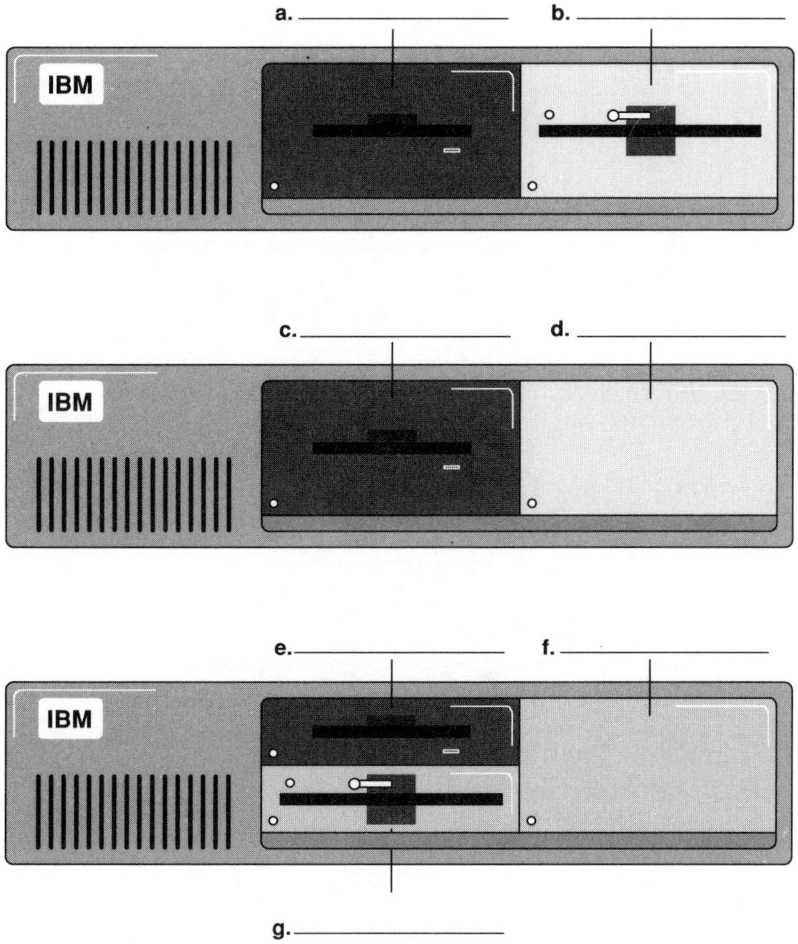

Figure 2 Disk drive configurations.

4. What type of system lets two or more programs execute concurrently? 4. ______________

5. What are the program blocks called in the virtual storage technique of paging? What are the corresponding memory spaces called? 5.a. ______________

b. ______________

6. A traditional user interface that requires users to remember commands: 6. ____________

7. Multiprogramming is considered to be ______ - driven 7. ____________

8. Having users take turns in a time-sharing environment is what type of scheduling? 8. ____________

9. In paging, what is needed to keep track of the various pages? 9. ____________

10. The generic operating system some consider a standard: 10. ____________

11. Which process of an operating system avoids interspersing the printout from several programs? 11. ____________

12. A program that overlays the operating system to provide a user friendly environment: 12. ____________

13. Identify a special case of multiprogramming that is not event driven. 13. ____________

14. The computer that pioneered a graphical user interface: 14. ____________

15. Another name for service programs: 15. ____________

16. What is it called when two programs each hold a resource that the other needs? 16. ____________

17. Identify the type of utility program that converts files from one form to another. What is a second type of utility program? **17.a.** ____________

b. ____________

18. In what are programs on the disk kept while waiting to be run? **18.** ____________

19. What causes normal processing to be suspended? **19.** ____________

20. A gesture-based user interface needs what kind of screen? **20.** ____________

21. What MS-DOS programs are kept on disk? **21.** ____________

22. The operating system process of keeping programs in memory separate is called **22.** ____________

23. Microsoft's graphical user interface is called: **23.** ____________

24. MS-DOS uses the > symbol as a **24.** ____________

25. Another name for the default drive is **25.** ____________

Test Answers

Multiple Choice

1. b	6. c	11. b	16. c	21. d
2. d	7. d	12. a	17. b	22. d
3. a	8. b	13. d	18. b	23. a
4. c	9. c	14. d	19. d	24. a
5. c	10. a	15. c	20. c	25. b

True/False

1. T	6. T	11. F	16. F	21. F
2. T	7. T	12. F	17. F	22. F
3. F	8. F	13. F	18. T	23. F
4. F	9. T	14. T	19. T	24. T
5. F	10. T	15. T	20. T	25. T

Matching I

1. e	6. j
2. d	7. f
3. h	8. b
4. a	9. c
5. i	10. g

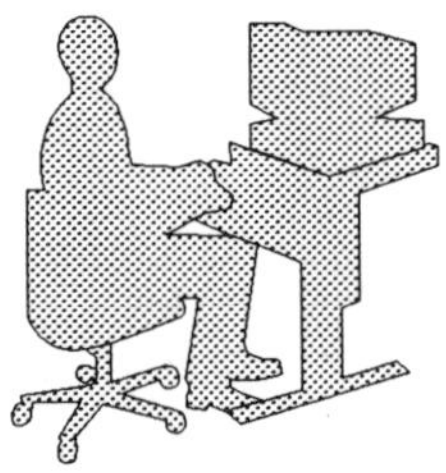

Matching II

1. e	6. d
2. c	7. i
3. h	8. f
4. a	9. b
5. j	10. g

Figures

Figure 1
a. user
b. applications programs
c. hardware
d. operating system

Figure 2
a. Drive A
b. Drive B
c. Drive A
d. Drive C
e. Drive A
f. Drive C
g. Drive B

Fill-In

1.a. control computer resources
  b. execute computer programs
  c. manage data

2. the supervisor program

3. response time

4. multiprogramming

5.a. pages
  b. page frames

6. command-line interface

7. event

8. round-robin

9. page table

10. UNIX

11. spooling

12. shell

13. time-sharing

14. Macintosh

15. utilities

16. deadlock

17.a. file handling
  b. sort/merge

18. queue

19. interrupt

20. touch sensitive

21. external

22. memory protection

23. Windows

24. prompt

25. current drive

Close to Home

Your principal connection with operating systems is likely to be the operating system you use when you use applications software such as word processing or spreadsheet packages on a personal computer. In this case, the commands you need to learn to interface with the operating system are not difficult.

CHAPTER

8

Systems Analysis and Design: Change and the Computer

Learning Objectives

- Understanding the terms *system*, *analysis*, and *design*.
- Understanding the nature of change theory.
- Knowing the principal functions of the systems analyst.
- Knowing the phases of the systems development life cycle.
- Familiarity with data gathering and analysis tools.
- Familiarity with systems design tools.
- Understanding the concept of prototyping.
- Understanding the value of CASE tools.

Why This Chapter Is Important

A career in programming? A career in business? Almost any path you travel may put you into direct contact with a systems analyst. Systems analysts have been trained to deal with users; now you, the user, have some training to deal with them.

Even if you do not deal directly with a systems analyst, you will most certainly use and be part of many computer-based business systems. You may be preparing input and you will receive and use output products. This chapter should give you a better understanding of the big picture, so you can place those inputs and outputs in context.

Chapter Outline

The Systems Analyst
- The Analyst and the System
- The Systems Analyst As Change Agent
- What It Takes to Be a Systems Analyst

How a Systems Analyst Works: Overview of the Systems Life Cycle

Phase 1: The Preliminary Investigation
- Problem Definition: Nature, Scope, Objectives
- Wrapping Up the Preliminary Investigation

Phase 2: Systems Analysis
- Data Gathering
- Data Analysis
- System Requirements
- Report to Management

Phase 3: Systems Design
- Preliminary Design
- Prototyping
- CASE Tools
- Detail Design

Phase 4: Systems Development
- Scheduling
- Programming
- Testing

Phase 5: Implementation
- Training
- Equipment Conversion
- File Conversion
- System Conversion
- Auditing
- Evaluation
- Maintenance

Putting It All Together: Is There a Formula?

Getting Personal with Computers

Key Words

Audit trail

Candidate

Change agent

Client

CASE

Computer system

Data analysis

Data flow diagram

Data gathering

Decision table

Direct conversion

Evaluation

Feasibility study

Gantt chart

Implementation

Observation

Organization chart

Parallel conversion

Participant observation

Phased conversion

Pilot conversion ____________________

Preliminary investigation ____________________

Printer spacing chart ____________________

Process ____________________

Programmer/analyst ____________________

Prototype ____________________

Questionnaire ____________________

Requirements ____________________

Sampling ____________________

Sink ____________________

Source ____________________

Structured interview ____________________

System ____________________

System journal ____________________

System survey ____________________

System testing ____________________

Systems analysis ____________________

Systems analyst ____________________

Systems design ____________________

Systems development ____________________

Systems development life cycle ____________________

Systems flowchart ____________________

Systems project ______________________
____
____

Unit testing ________________________
____
____

Unstructured interview ______________
____
____

User involvement ____________________
____
____

Vector ______________________________
____
____

Volume testing ______________________
____
____

SAVE A TREE

Over the years, systems analysts have made mighty efforts to separate users from paper by having them display information on a computer screen instead; one analyst suggested that it is easier to get a security blanket away from a baby.

Nordstrom, Inc., a Seattle-based department store, has made strides in this area by tying its efforts to the environment. In addition to telling workers how much paper they are saving and how many trees that represents, the company plants a tree for each percentage point of paper reduction.

Study Hints

The most important parts of the chapter are the phases of a systems project. To gain a more thorough understanding of the process, you should follow the accompanying case study carefully.

THE COMPUTER AS INTERVIEWER

When people are nervous in interview situations they may show themselves poorly or may become completely tongue-tied. Given this situation, do you think they would prefer talking to a machine? The surprising answer is yes. Another aspect of the preference for machines - computers - is that the machine is perceived as being more impersonal and therefore less threatening.

Self-Test

Multiple Choice

1. Testing of each individual program or module is called
   a. program testing
   b. system testing
   c. volume testing
   d. unit testing

2. The preliminary investigation of a systems project is also called a(n)
   a. analysis survey
   b. feasibility study
   c. systems design
   d. evaluation

3. The people who will have contact with the system, such as employees and customers, are
   a. shoppers
   b. users
   c. systems analysts
   d. planners

4. The SDLC is defined as a project involving
   a. two phases
   b. three phases
   c. four phases
   d. five phases

5. Phase one of a systems project involves
   a. a system survey
   b. a systems analysis
   c. data gathering
   d. questionnaires

6. The person who fills the role of change agent is the
   a. systems user
   b. administrator
   c. systems analyst
   d. client

7. The scope and true nature of the problem is determined during
   a. the second phase
   b. the systems development
   c. the preliminary investigation
   d. the systems analysis

8. A chart of positions and departments within an organization is a(n)
   a. data flow diagram
   b. organization chart
   c. record layout
   d. Gantt chart

9. In a data flow diagram, a destination for data outside the organization is called a
   a. vector
   b. source
   c. file
   d. sink

10. In the course of a systems project, systems design
    a. follows systems analysis
    b. precedes systems analysis
    c. follows development
    d. is the fourth phase

11. Positioning of headings and columns for the report format, considered during systems design, might use a(n)
    a. record layout
    b. decision table
    c. organization chart
    d. printer spacing chart

12. Scheduling, programming, testing, and documentation are elements of
    a. systems analysis
    b. implementation
    c. systems development
    d. systems design

13. Data gathering and data analysis take place
    a. after the system survey
    b. during systems design
    c. after systems analysis
    d. during evaluation

14. The kind of interview where all questions are planned in advance is called
    a. pre-planned
    b. observation
    c. structured
    d. unstructured

15. The entire new system is used by a portion of the users:
    a. direct conversion
    b. file conversion
    c. pilot conversion
    d. parallel conversion

16. A systems analyst would observe the flow of data and interrelations of people within an organization during
    a. detail design
    b. systems analysis
    c. preliminary design
    d. a system survey

17. Used to ensure that no alternative is overlooked during data analysis:
    a. data flow diagram
    b. Gantt chart
    c. organization chart
    d. decision table

18. The phase following detail design is
    a. preliminary investigation
    b. systems development
    c. implementation
    d. system conversion

19. The process by which old files are converted to make them accessible to the new computer system is called
    a. phased conversion
    b. pilot conversion
    c. parallel conversion
    d. file conversion

20. Training and maintenance are elements of
    a. systems design
    b. preliminary investigation
    c. implementation
    d. systems development

21. The person who requests study or work on a system is the
    a. client
    b. change agent
    c. analyst
    d. user

22. The data gathering vehicle that permits high-volume anonymous answers:
    a. observation
    b. questionnaire
    c. unstructured interview
    d. structured interview

23. In the preliminary design phase, the analyst prepares alternative
    a. candidates
    b. questionnaires
    c. organization charts
    d. decision tables

24. A set of tools for automated design is called
    a. prototypes
    b. CASE
    c. data flow diagrams
    d. Gantt charts

25. A plan to trace data to its source is called
    a. an audit trail
    b. sampling
    c. a vector
    d. volume testing

True/False

T F 1. Systems analysis is the process of developing a plan for an approved system.

T F 2. Users are people who will have contact with the system.

T F 3. A systems analyst normally performs both analysis and design.

T F 4. Documentation is the least important aspect of a systems project.

T F 5. A feasibility study needs to be conducted following data gathering.

T F 6. Questionnaires are usually a more expensive form of data gathering than are interviews.

T F 7. An organization chart shows the flow of data through an organization.

T F 8. A decision table can help ensure that no alternative is overlooked.

T F 9. A report to management should be presented following the systems analysis phase.

T F 10. Input requirements should be considered prior to considering output requirements.

T F 11. Problem definition includes the nature of the problem, its scope, and the objectives of the system.

T F 12. Prototyping tools include powerful high-level software.

T F 13. Source documents should be serially numbered and accounted for during the system control step of systems design.

T F 14. A systems flowchart is the same as a logic flowchart.

T F 15. A Gantt chart is a bar chart to depict deadlines and milestones.

T F 16. Programming, testing, and documentation take place primarily during implementation.

T F 17. File conversion is one form of system conversion.

T F 18. Maintenance of the system should take only a short time if the previous work was done with care.

T F 19. Poor communication between analysts and users can result in a system that does not do what the user expected.

T F 20. CASE tools permit both automated design and automated revision of a system.

T F 21. Even if unit testing is done thoroughly, system testing is necessary.

T F 22. Most people are uncomfortable with change.

T F 23. Input to on-line systems should be backed up with system journals.

T F 24. A phased conversion is riskier than a direct conversion.

T F 25. A source is a data origin outside the organization.

Matching I

___ 1. system survey
___ 2. data gathering
___ 3. prototype
___ 4. parallel conversion
___ 5. printer spacing chart
___ 6. user relationships
___ 7. audit trail
___ 8. Gantt chart
___ 9. system processing
___ 10. system control

a. questionnaire, interview
b. report format
c. schedule deadlines
d. numbered source documents
e. systems flowchart
f. data trace
g. feasibility study
h. concurrent operation
i. organization chart
j. limited system

Matching II

___ 1. automated design
___ 2. fastest conversion
___ 3. users
___ 4. processes
___ 5. candidates
___ 6. systems analysis
___ 7. scope
___ 8. ballot box
___ 9. systems development
___ 10. volume testing

a. direct
b. real data
c. programming, testing
d. gather and analyze data
e. alternative plans
f. check yes or no
g. CASE tools
h. employees, customers
i. boundaries
j. actions on data

Fill-In

1. What is the process called that evaluates a presently existing system to determine how it works and how it meets user needs? 1. ____________

2. List the three principal functions of a systems analyst.
   2.a. ____________
   b. ____________
   c. ____________

3. What means is used to illustrate information flow within an organization? 3. ____________

4. What is the first step of the systems analysis phase of a systems project? The second step?
   4.a. ____________
   b. ____________

5. What is the total procedure to develop a new project through the five phases called? 5. ____________

6. Who is the person or the organization that contracts to have a systems analysis done? 6. ____________

7. What are files whose records represent transactions made by on-line systems? 7. ____________

8. Place in order the five parts of the system considered during detail systems design.

8.a. ____________________

b. ____________________

c. ____________________

d. ____________________

e. ____________________

9. Because a systems analyst brings change to an organization, what is the analyst often referred to as?

9. ____________________

10. What is the by-product of understanding the system in the systems analysis phase?

10. ____________________

11. List five sources of information for data gathering.

11.a. ____________________

b. ____________________

c. ____________________

d. ____________________

e. ____________________

12. In data flow diagrams, what is the name for a repository of data?

12. ____________________

13. Auditing, evaluation, and maintenance are part of which phase?

13. ____________________

14. Which method of conversion is the most prolonged and expensive?

14. ____________________

15. Name two other terms for the preliminary investigation.

15.a. ____________

b. ____________

16. List, in order, the five phases of a systems project.

16.a. ____________

b. ____________

c. ____________

d. ____________

e. ____________

17. Gathering a representative data subset is called:

17. ____________

18. What are alternative plans for a new system design called?

18. ____________

19. During which phase should programming begin?

19. ____________

20. What word describes an organized set of related components that accomplish a certain task?

20. ____________

TAKING YOUR MONEY

Many computer systems take direct aim at the consumer. Some recent approaches are in-store interactive video shopping, light-'em-up electronic shelf tags, debit cards that instantly reach your bank account, and even self-checkout.

Test Answers

Multiple Choice

1. d	6. c	11. d	16. b	21. a
2. b	7. c	12. c	17. d	22. b
3. b	8. b	13. a	18. b	23. a
4. d	9. d	14. c	19. d	24. b
5. a	10. a	15. c	20. c	25. a

True/False

1. F	6. F	11. T	16. F	21. T
2. T	7. F	12. T	17. F	22. T
3. T	8. T	13. T	18. F	23. T
4. F	9. T	14. F	19. T	24. F
5. F	10. F	15. T	20. F	25. T

Matching I

1. g	6. i
2. a	7. f
3. j	8. c
4. h	9. e
5. b	10. d

Matching II

1. g	6. d
2. a	7. i
3. h	8. f
4. j	9. c
5. e	10. b

Fill-In

1. systems analysis

2.a. coordination
 b. communication
 c. planning and design

3. data flow diagram

4.a. data gathering
 b. data analysis

5. SDLC

6. the client

7. system journals

8.a. output requirements
 b. input
 c. files and databases
 d. system processing
 e. system controls, backup

9. change agent

10. requirements

11.a. written documents
 b. questionnaires
 c. interviews
 d. observation
 e. sampling

12. file

13. implementation

14. parallel conversion

15.a. feasibility study
 b. system survey

16.a. preliminary
 b. systems analysis
 c. systems design
 d. systems development
 e. implementation

17. sampling

18. candidates

19. systems development

20. system

Close to Home

As you have seen in the chapter, the systems analysis process introduces change. All of us, systems analysts or otherwise, will be affected in some way by computer-introduced changes. How will we handle those changes? The answer may be related to how we handle changes in our daily lives now; some of us are flexible, some less so. It is an interesting experiment to introduce changes to your own life and observe your responses: take a different route to school, study in a different place, change your hairstyle. These changes are rather minor, but many people have difficulty making them smoothly. Another point to keep in mind: Some people manage their own self-introduced changes pretty well but react negatively if it is someone else's idea.

CHAPTER

9

Word Processing and Desktop Publishing: The Most Popular Software on Personal Computers

Learning Objectives

- ❑ Appreciation of the need for word processing.
- ❑ Understanding the basic features of word processing programs.
- ❑ Familiarization with the standard programs that are related to word processing: spelling checkers, thesaurus programs, and programs for grammar and style, and form letters.
- ❑ Appreciating the advantages of desktop publishing.
- ❑ Understanding desktop publishing terminology.
- ❑ Understanding hardware and software requirements for desktop publishing.

Why This Chapter Is Important

It is hard to imagine what computer-related topic could be more important for your future in *any* career than word processing. Perhaps beyond this, it is a very definite personal convenience. We have noticed, in the past few years, that some people actually avoid tasks that they should do because they have also avoided word processing and cannot face using a typewriter. (There are also people who avoid word processing because they cannot type.) They often recognize that they have a self-imposed handicap and are embarrassed about it. Word processing is foundational.

However, your career will probably not flourish or languish based on your level of desktop publishing knowledge. But a rudimentary understanding of desktop publishing is advantageous for anyone who will be working in an office.

Chapter Outline

Word Processing as a Tool

An Overview:
How Word Processing Works
- Scrolling
- No Need to Worry About the Right Side
- Easy Corrections
- Function Keys: Making It Easy

Getting Started: Using a Word Processing Package
- Loading the Program
- Creating the Cover Letter
  - Entering the Letter
  - Saving the Letter
  - Printing the Letter
  - Exiting the Program
- Editing the Letter
  - Retrieving the Letter
  - Making the Changes
  - Saving the Corrected Letter

Formatting: Making A Good Impression
- The Resume Example
- Adding Blank Lines
- Centering Lines
- Vertical Centering
- Changing Margins
- Justifying the Right Margin
- Adding Boldface and Underlining
- Reveal Codes

Text Blocks
- The Survey Example
- Marking a Block
- Moving a Block
- Deleting a Block
- Copying a Block

Help!

I have a spelling checker.
It came with my PC.
It plainly marks four my revue
Mistake I cannot see.
I ran this program threw it,
I'm sure your please two no.
It's letter perfect in it's weigh,
My checker tolled me sew.

This little ditty, circulating among office workers, shows how a spelling checker can make people look dumb. Moral of the story: the spelling checker can indeed help, but human checkers must also help themselves.

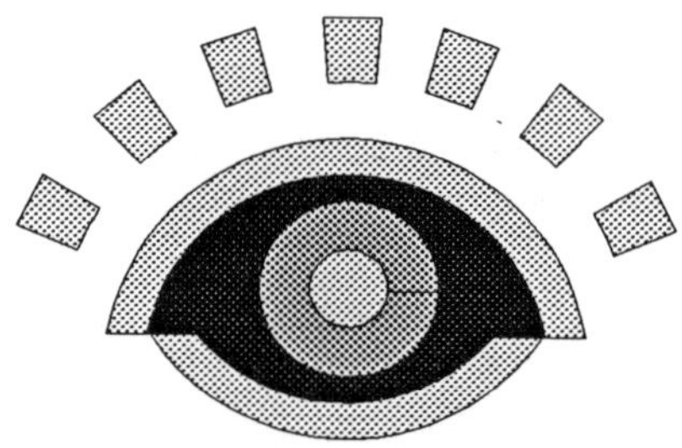

WINK WINK

Well, actually, it's blink, blink. Blinking is what you should be doing as you sit at the screen. Unfortunately, researchers have discovered that video display workers tend to get dry scratchy eyes because they don't blink enough. Although people blink at the rate of 18.4 blinks per minute while talking, the average worker blinks only 3.6 times per minute when looking at the screen. So, blink more often.

CRUISE AND COMPUTE

So you want to take a cruise. Blue seas, balmy nights, classy entertainment - and computers. Is there no escape from technology? Well, guess what: The passengers on the five-star cruise ship *Queen Elizabeth II* love it. A shipboard room completely filled with IBM Personal Computers is available, along with a wide range of software packages. Each station also includes a printer.

And just what are the passengers doing with the machines on their vacations? Plotting business decisions? Checking profits? Some are. But most are using word processing for writing letters and keeping travel diaries. One woman wrote a complete novel during her trip around the world.

BENDING AND TWISTING

If you are even thinking about word processing, much less desktop publishing, then it is assumed that you can type. But, as many researchers have shown, today's keyboard is not particularly suited for the way people naturally move their hands. Try this: put your hands out in front of you as if you were typing. Now rotate your hands so that the thumbs are pointing up, and keep typing. Feel better? Some people think so. In fact, manufacturers are now producing keyboards that *bend* into shape so you can type with your thumbs up. Weird? Yes. Comfortable? Also, yes. Stay tuned.

Key Words

Automatic reformatting ____________________

Block copy ____________________

Block delete ____________________

Block move ____________________

Boldface ____________________

Camera-ready ____________________

Centering ____________________

Conditional replace ____________________

Cursor ____________________

Cursor movement keys ____________________

Default settings ____________________

Desktop publishing ____________________

Desktop publishing programs ____________________

Desktop publishing templates ____________________

Electronic publishing ____________________

Font ____________________

Font library ____________________

Form letter program ____________________

Format ____________________

Grammar and style program ____________________

Halftone ______________________

Help ______________________

Imagesetter ______________________

Internal fonts ______________________

Insert mode ______________________

Justified text ______________________

Kerning ______________________

Leading ______________________

Marked block ______________________

Menu ______________________

Page composition ______________________

Page description language (PDL) ______________________

Page layout ______________________

Page makeup programs ______________________

Point ______________________

Ragged-right margin ______________________

Reveal codes ______________________

Reverse video ______________________

Right margin ______________________

Scrolling ______________________

Search and replace ______________________

Soft font ______________________

Spelling checker program ____________

Style ____________

Table of contents program ____________

Text block ____________

Thesaurus program ____________

Toggle switch ____________

Type face ____________

Type size ____________

Typeover mode ____________

Typeset quality ____________

Underline ____________

Vertical centering ____________

Weight ____________

Word processing ____________

Word wrap ____________

WYSIWYG ____________

Study Hints

This is easy. Get your hands on a word processing program and practice. However, if you are fortunate enough to have access to desktop publishing software, you will need training beyond the scope of this chapter. All that is required in this chapter is familiarity with the special terms associated with desktop publishing.

Self-Test

Multiple Choice

1. A set of choices on the screen is called a(an)
   a. menu
   b. reverse video
   c. editor
   d. template

2. A program that provides synonyms is called a(n)
   a. indexing program
   b. form letter program
   c. editing program
   d. thesaurus program

3. An electronically-produced form letter is called a
   a. scroll
   b. block
   c. menu
   d. boilerplate

4. A program that can identify unnecessary words and wordy phrases is called a(n)
   a. indexing program
   b. form letter program
   c. editing program
   d. thesaurus program

5. The feature that keeps track of the right margin is
   a. search and replace
   b. word wrap
   c. ragged right
   d. right justified

6. If using verification with the search and replace feature, this is called
   a. verified replace
   b. conditional replace
   c. questionable replace
   d. what-if replace

7. The feature that allows viewing any part of a document on the screen is
   a. searching
   b. scrolling
   c. pasting
   d. editing

8. The command to transfer text to another location without deleting it from its original location is
   a. scroll
   b. search
   c. copy
   d. move

9. Ragged right means the right margin is set to be
   a. uneven
   b. variable
   c. even
   d. wide

10. Spelling checker programs use
a. tab settings
b. function keys
c. boilerplating
d. a dictionary

True/False

T F 1. Formatting refers to adjusting the appearance of a document to make it look attractive and appropriate.

T F 2. Scrolling lets a user see about 40 lines of text at the screen.

T F 3. A spelling checker program can detect spelling typos, and improper use of language.

T F 4. Right justified means that the right margin will be ragged right.

T F 5. The move command moves text to another place and deletes it from its original place.

T F 6. A form letter program uses a boilerplate.

T F 7. The common feature of word processing and typing is permanent marks made on paper as the document is keyed.

T F 8. In word processing, a file is a computer-created document.

T F 9. The copy command moves text to another place and deletes it from its original place.

T F 10. A thesaurus program can be used to create a table of contents.

T F 11. A grammar and style program is also called an editing program.

T F 12. Text is centered vertically by adjusting the right margin.

T F 13. A conditional replace goes through the program and replaces each instance of a repeated error.

T F 14. The Del key acts as a toggle switch.

T F 15. Text can be marked to be underlined when printed.

T F **16.** The paper or plastic form which fits over the keys to describe their use is called a template.

T F **17.** Word processing is the creation, editing, storing, and printing of text.

T F **18.** You can move up an entire page, as it would be printed, using the PgUp key.

T F **19.** The feature that removes user control of the right side of the document is the tab setting.

T F **20.** The cursor is usually a blinking dash or rectangle.

T F **21.** The quality of the monitor is important for desktop publishing.

T F **22.** Graphics capability is not required for desktop publishing.

T F **23.** Most desktop publishing systems include an inexpensive dot-matrix printer.

T F **24.** The larger the dots that a printer can produce, the higher the resolution.

T F **25.** For most companies, printing costs are a relatively small part of the budget.

T F **26.** Printer quality is important for camera-ready output.

T F **27.** Desktop publishing is suitable for most in-house publications.

T F **28.** Few businesses today can afford desktop publishing.

T F **29.** Imagesetters usually print at lower resolutions.

T F **30.** Text printed at a higher resolution is more readable than text printed at a lower resolution.

T F **31.** Another name for a page composition program is page makeup program.

T F **32.** Once a page layout has been planned using desktop publishing, it is very difficult to change.

T F **33.** Resolution of 2540 dots per inch is considered top-of-the line typeset quality.

T F **34.** Most desktop publishing software programs do not have their own fonts.

T F **35.** Kerning refers to the space between lines.

T F **36.** Adding type to a page layout is called leading.

T F **37.** Once a size and style have been selected for headings, they must be used consistently throughout the publication.

T F **38.** It is possible to do desktop publishing on a personal computer.

T F **39.** A point is approximately one-quarter inch.

T F **40.** Halftones are made up of black, grey, and white dots.

OLYMPICS PAPER

Instead of relying on an off-site print shop or newspaper publisher, the folks at the Olympic games produce their daily newspaper right on the Olympics grounds, using desktop publishing and personal computers. The computers are linked to each other and to color printers. The final product is often several dozen pages.

The concept of a portable newspaper is catching on for coverage of disasters or special events such as political conventions. Such papers have even been used in war zones, where, as one wag put it, high terror meets high tech.

Matching I

___	1. cut and paste	a. default
___	2. word wrap	b. find and correct
___	3. file	c. form letter
___	4. thesaurus program	d. reorder text
___	5. boldface	e. synonyms
___	6. editing program	f. computer-created document
___	7. function keys	g. grammar and style
___	8. boilerplate	h. print darker
___	9. original setting	i. watches right margin
___	10. search and replace	j. execute common commands

Matching II

___	1. measured by point	a. leading
___	2. spacing between lines	b. template
___	3. desktop publishing	c. page layout
___	4. prepared page layout	d. type size
___	5. space between characters	e. clip art
___	6. art stored on disk	f. halftone
___	7. resin-coated paper	g. resolution
___	8. image of dots	h. electronic publishing
___	9. arrangement on page	i. kerning
___	10. image clarity	j. imagesetters

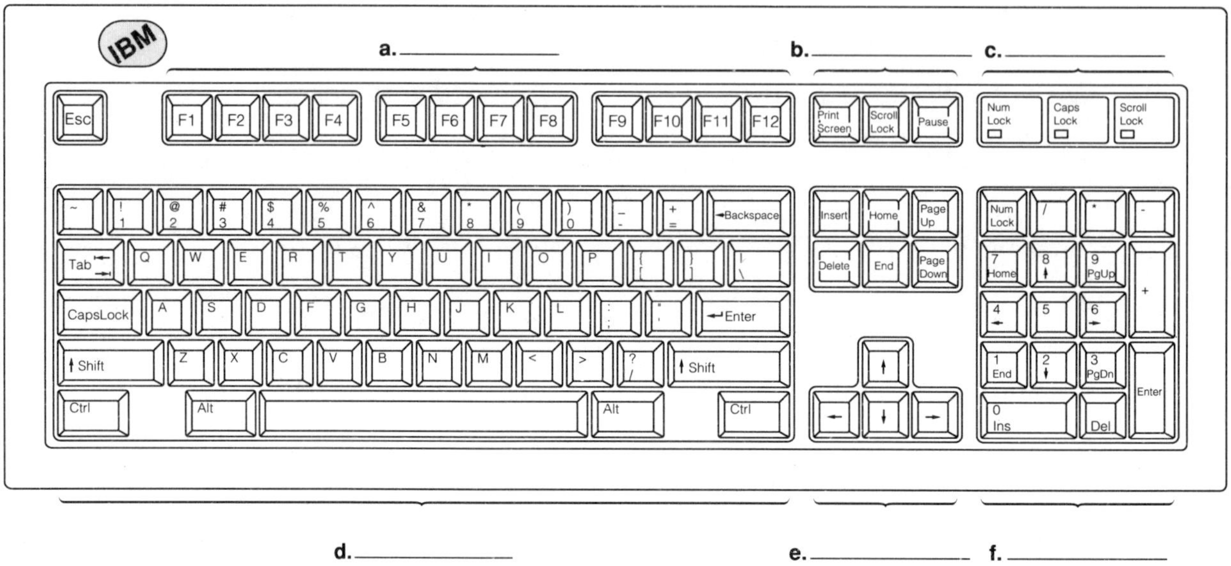

Figure 1 Keyboard.

Fill-In

1. What is an electronic form letter called? 1. ____________
2. What is a word processing program that presents an on-screen menu said to be? 2. ____________
3. What kind of commands are copy and move commands generally known as? 3. ____________
4. Which feature permits a user to view any part of a document, about 20 lines at a time? 4. ____________
5. Resetting what will make a document shorter and wider? 5. ____________

6. Which feature finds and changes text? 6. ____________

7. What are words printed in darker type said to be? 7. ____________

8. Before a block of text can be copied or moved, what must be done first? 8. ____________

9. An even right margin is said to be: 9. ____________

10. What is the verification feature with search and replace called? 10. ____________

11. A complete set of characters in a particular size, typeface, weight, and style is called: 11. ____________

12. A set of drawings stored on disk: 12. ____________

13. Printers used for desktop publishing must have what software on a ROM chip? 13. ____________

14. The fonts stored in the printer are called: 14. ____________

15. Adding type to a layout is called: 15. ____________

16. A sheet that is ready to be photographed to make a plate for printing is said to be: 16. ____________

17. Italic is an example of what typeface characteristic? 17. ____________

18. Boldface is an example of what typeface characteristic? 18. ____________

19. A set of characters of the same design: 19. ____________

20. Very high resolution is called: 20. ____________

Test Answers

Multiple Choice

1. a	6. b
2. d	7. b
3. d	8. c
4. c	9. a
5. b	10. d

True/False

1. T	6. T	11. T	16. T
2. F	7. F	12. F	17. T
3. F	8. T	13. F	18. T
4. F	9. F	14. F	19. F
5. T	10. F	15. T	20. T

21. T	26. T	31. T	36. F
22. F	27. T	32. F	37. F
23. F	28. F	33. T	38. T
24. F	29. F	34. F	39. F
25. F	30. T	35. F	40. F

Matching I

1. d	6. g
2. i	7. j
3. f	8. c
4. e	9. a
5. h	10. b

Matching II

1. d	6. e
2. a	7. j
3. h	8. f
4. b	9. c
5. i	10. g

Figure

Figure 1

a. function keys
b. additional keys
c. status lights
d. main keyboard
e. cursor movement keys
f. numeric keys

Fill-In

1. boilerplate
2. menu driven
3. cut and paste
4. scrolling
5. margins
6. search and replace
7. boldface
8. mark the text
9. justified
10. conditional replace
11. font
12. clip art
13. page description language
14. internal fonts
15. page composition
16. camera ready
17. style
18. weight
19. typeface
20. typeset quality

Close to Home

The debate about who needs a personal computer - and why - rages on. However, for many people, the answer is very clear: A personal computer is worthwhile for word processing alone. But many people choose to go a step further, into the realm of desktop publishing. This becomes clearer each day, as our mailboxes are stuffed with fancy club newsletters and even family letters with computer-generated artwork.

CHAPTER

10

Spreadsheets: What if . . . .

Learning Objectives

- ❑ Appreciating the need for spreadsheets.
- ❑ Familiarization with the development of the electronic spreadsheet.
- ❑ Understanding the underlying principles of electronic spreadsheet use.
- ❑ Acquaintance with the electronic spreadsheet package Lotus 1-2-3.
- ❑ Understanding the nature of integrated packages, and their advantages and disadvantages.
- ❑ Appreciating the different types of graphics programs and the equipment required.

Why This Chapter Is Important

Many business people use spreadsheets to plan and monitor activities. The terminology of spreadsheets is becoming part of everyday business. Even if you do not prepare or use spreadsheets in your job, you may have to understand and analyze the spreadsheets someone else has prepared. At the very least, you will probably be exposed to them and you will want to know what they are.

Computer-produced graphics are being used by people in diverse aspects of business. Even if you do not use them yourself, you will at least be seeing them in the business world.

Chapter Outline

Electronic Spreadsheets

Spreadsheet Fundamentals
- Cells and Cell Addresses
- Contents of Cells
- Ranges
- Moving the Cursor
- Operating Modes
- The Control Panel
- Menus and Submenus

Creating A Simple Spreadsheet
- The Expense Sheet Example
- Loading the Program
- Entering the Labels and Values
- Entering the Formulas and Functions
- Making Corrections

Using Spreadsheet Commands
- The File Command
- The Print Command
- The Worksheet Erase Command
- The Quit Command

Using the Help Key

Integrated Packages
- The First Integrated Package
- To Integrate or Not?

Business Graphics
- Why Use Graphics?
- Analytical Graphics
- Presentation Graphics

Some Business Graphics Terminology
- Line Graphs
- Bar Graphs
- Pie Charts

On to Storing Data

Questions & Answers

GETTING YOUR QUESTIONS ANSWERED

You bought the new software package you wanted, but now you have a problem using it. If you are by yourself at home or being a pioneer at the office, you may want to resort to the help lines established by the software vendor. If you can get through, that is. People sometimes spend hours trying to get through to the customer-service people.

And what about the customer-service representatives? There are lots of them, 40 or 50 at places like Microsoft and Lotus. But they cannot keep up with the torrent of calls. The problem, you see, is rarely faulty software or obscure documentation; most callers are too lazy to look it up in the documentation they have available. Software manufacturers want to be helpful, but if they are too helpful the overhead costs can exceed the cost the user paid for the software.

This knotty little problem is being solved in several ways. Some manufacturers have only mail-order assistance on certain products. Others allow a certain number of phone calls per registered software and then charge a fee. Borland International runs a forum on the CompuServe network, where customer questions can be answered by either the company's technicians or by other users. As you might suspect, in all cases where users have to pay, their queries have diminished significantly.

Key Words

Active cell ______________________________

Analytical graphics ______________________________

Axis ______________________________

Data point ______________________________

Cell ______________________________

Cell address ______________________________

Cell contents ______________________________

Clip art ______________________________

Clustered-bar graph ______________________________

Command menu ______________________________

Command tree ______________________________

Control panel ______________________________

Current cell ______________________________

Displayed value ______________________________

Electronic spreadsheet ______________________________

Entry mode ______________________________

Exploded pie chart ______________________________

Formula ______________________________

Function ______________________________

GoTo function key ______________________________

Graphics adapter board ____________

Graphics card ____________

Graphics printer ____________

Help key ____________

Integrated package ____________

Jump-To function key ____________

Legend ____________

Line graph ____________

Lotus 1-2-3 ____________

Menu mode ____________

Mode ____________

Mode indicator ____________

Multiple-range graph ____________

Pie chart ____________

Pixel ____________

Plot area ____________

Pointer ____________

Presentation graphics ____________

Range ____________

Ready mode ____________

Single-range graph ____________

Spreadsheet ____________

Stacked-bar graph ____________________
____
____

Stand-alone program __________________
____
____

Submenu ______________________________
____
____

Title ________________________________
____
____

Universal manager program ____________
____
____

Variable _____________________________
____
____

X-axis _______________________________
____
____

Y-axis _______________________________
____
____

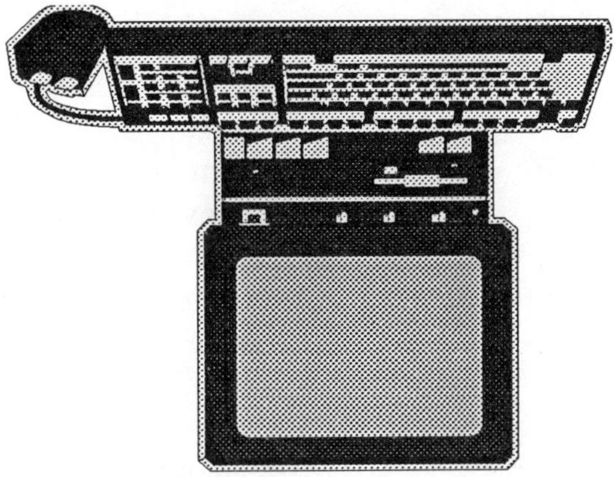

STUPID COMPUTER TRICKS

No, these programs will not make your computer stand on its head, but they do offer some "insanely great" tricks, such as playing all four verses of the Star Spangled Banner or generating a cheerful compliment as a user turns the computer on. But most people like to use these programs to play tricks on their unsuspecting friends. One scam randomly selects a character on the screen, say the letter m, and replaces it with one just like it, but in a different color. All these little tricks, we hasten to add, are harmless. Interested? Look for the book, with disks, by LeVitus and Tittel.

Study Hints

Most schools have some spreadsheet packages available for student use. If possible, direct participation is the best path to follow.

Self-Test

True/False

T F **1.** The program credited with helping Apple's early success is Lotus 1-2-3.

T F **2.** Templates are spreadsheets with all the commands, labels, and formulas already entered.

T F **3.** Stand-alone programs can be integrated by a universal manager program.

T F **4.** A manual spreadsheet is capable of automatically recalculating totals when changes are made to figures in the spreadsheet.

T F **5.** Integrated packages are very inexpensive, although you still pay for all the functions in the package, even if you need only some of them.

T F **6.** Programs that share a common methodology and command structure are called stand-alone.

T F **7.** Individual functions, like word processing, within integrated packages are not usually as strong as those in stand-alone packages.

T F **8.** The first integrated package was Lotus 1-2-3.

T F **9.** The Dickens clerk example was of an electronic spreadsheet.

T F **10.** The first electronic spreadsheet was VisiCalc.

T F **11.** Analytical graphics let you construct line, bar, and pie chart graphs.

T F **12.** Many presentation graphics can edit and enhance charts created by other programs.

T F **13.** Presentation graphics appear professionally produced.

T F **14.** Column widths in Lotus spreadsheets are fixed.

T F **15.** Analytical graphics use a library of symbols to enhance output.

T F **16.** The active spreadsheet cell is marked by the pointer.

T F **17.** Labels identify categories along graph axes.

T F **18.** On an exploded pie chart, one wedge is slightly removed from the pie for emphasis.

T F **19.** A spreadsheet HELP key is context sensitive, meaning that it offers information related to the command being used.

T F **20.** In a spreadsheet, a label cannot be used for calculations.

Matching

___	**1.** legend	a. stand-alone
___	**2.** separate software	b. one variable
___	**3.** simple graphics	c. analytical
___	**4.** many variables	d. label, number, formula
___	**5.** cell	e. spreadsheet
___	**6.** cell data	f. graph explanation
___	**7.** enhanced graphics	g. current cell
___	**8.** worksheet	h. presentation
___	**9.** pie chart	i. location on spreadsheet
___	**10.** active cell	j. multiple-range graph

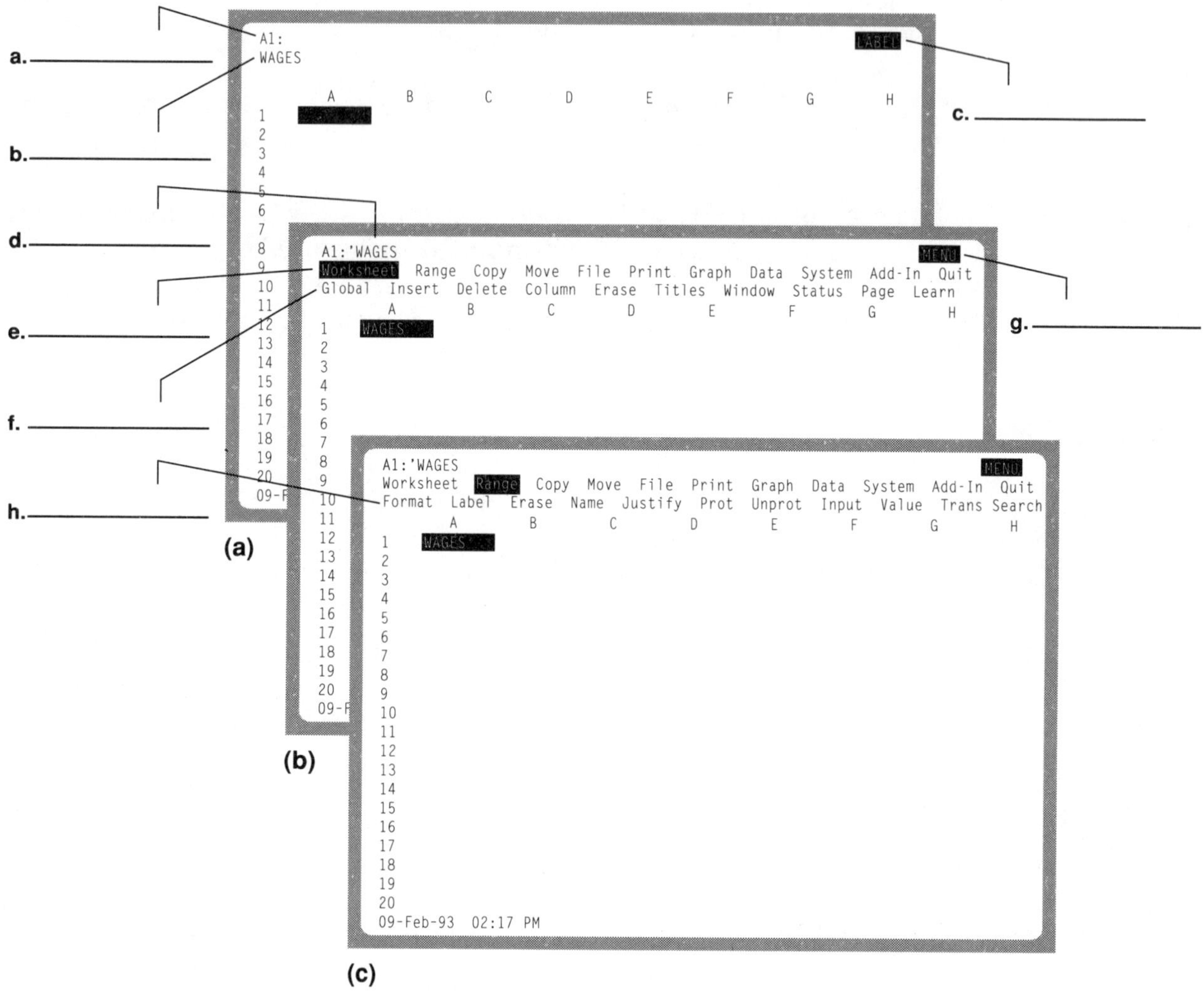

Figure 1 The Lotus 1-2-3 control panel.

Fill-In

1. List the three types of information Lotus lets a user enter in a spreadsheet cell. 1.a. ____________________

   b. ____________________

   c. ____________________

2. The screen entries Range, Copy, Move, and Print are part of what type of Lotus menu? 2. ____________________

3. What are enhanced graphics called? 3. ____________________

4. In a spreadsheet, a formula or function is called the cell content; what is the calculated result called? 4. ____________________

5. What is the intersection of a row and column on a spreadsheet called? 5. ____________________

6. Plain line graphs are an example of what kind of graphics? 6. ____________________

7. The user can see any part of a spreadsheet by using which keys? 7. ____________________

8. Another name for the active cell: 8. ____________________

9. What are spreadsheets with all the commands, labels, and formulas already entered called? 9. ____________________

10. A preprogrammed formula is called: 10. ____________________

Test Answers

True/False

1. F	6. F	11. T	16. T
2. T	7. T	12. T	17. T
3. T	8. T	13. T	18. T
4. F	9. F	14. F	19. T
5. F	10. T	15. F	20. T

Matching

1. f	6. d
2. a	7. h
3. c	8. e
4. j	9. b
5. i	10. g

Figure

Figure 1

a. status line
b. key-in text
c. ENTRY mode
d. contents of cell A1
e. command menu
f. submenu for Worksheet command
g. MENU mode
h. submenu for Range command

Fill-In

1.a. labels
 b. numbers
 c. formulas

2. command

3. presentation

4. displayed value

5. cell

6. analytical

7. cursor control keys

8. current cell

9. templates

10. function

Close to Home

The use of spreadsheets at home is not for everyone. But if you are interested, there are applications. A spreadsheet can give you better insight into your personal budget or investments. Some people use spreadsheets for sports-related statistics, others to monitor personal practices such as exercise habits.

CHAPTER

11

Database Management Systems: Getting Data Together

Learning Objectives

- ❑ Appreciating the advantages of databases.
- ❑ Understanding how databases are organized.
- ❑ Acquaintance with dBASE IV.
- ❑ General understanding of how to build and change a database.

Why This Chapter Is Important

Along with word processing and spreadsheets, databases are a key business application of personal computers. But, unlike word processing and spreadsheets, databases are also used extensively on larger computers. It is likely that you will be using databases, directly or indirectly, in your career.

Chapter Outline

Key Words

Attribute ______________________

Catalog ______________________

Character field ______________________

Control Center ______________________

Data item ______________________

Database ______________________

Database management system (DBMS) ______________________

Date field ______________________

Dot prompt ______________________

Field name ______________________

Field type ______________________

Field width ______________________

File ______________________

Floating point field ______________________

Logical field ______________________

Memo field ______________________

Model ______________________

Numeric field ______________________

Pan ______________________

Query ______________________

Quick report ______________________
____
____

Record ______________________
____
____

Relation ______________________
____
____

Relational operator ______________________
____
____

Relational database ______________________
____
____

Selection bar ______________________
____
____

Tuple ______________________
____
____

Worksurface ______________________
____
____

Study Hints

As always with software, the best way to learn about databases and how they work is to experiment with database software on a personal computer.

HERE COMES THE JUDGE, WITH A COMPUTER

To the intonation "All rise," the judge arrives in flowing black robes and perches on the bench. But what is that next to the judge? A computer - right there on the bench!

Judges are finding computers in court highly functional. Databases provide information about which defendants are to appear before the court that day, and data including aliases, probation history, and previous convictions. There has been a curious sidenote to all this: with the "know all" machine right there in plain sight, suspects have become more truthful in court.

Self-Test

True/False

T F **1.** A logical operator, such as =, <, or >, is needed when making comparisons in dBASE III PLUS.

T F **2.** In dBASE IV, commands must be entered via the dot prompt.

T F **3.** Databases reduce data redundancy.

T F **4.** A database is a collection of data prepared for a particular user in separate files.

T F **5.** The pan operation moves sideways across the screen so all fields in a database can be viewed.

T F **6.** Two key benefits of database processing are shared data and segregated files.

T F **7.** One disadvantage of databases is that they can be used by only a single user.

T F **8.** There are two steps to creating a file, designing the structure of the file and entering the data.

T F **9.** Database models represent data relationships found in the real world.

T F **10.** Databases tend to decentralize data.

T F **11.** The database model most commonly used on personal computers is the hierarchical model.

T F **12.** dBASE IV uses the relational model.

T F **13.** In dBASE IV, deleting records is a two-step process.

T F **14.** In dBASE IV, records can be modified with the Edit screen or the Browse screen.

T F **15.** An attribute is a column of a relation.

T F **16.** A tuple is a row of a relation.

T F **17.** In dBASE IV, the most important menu is the Control Center.

T F **18.** In dBASE IV, the field width is not adjustable.

T F **19.** In dBASE IV, menus are called work surfaces.

T F **20.** In dBASE IV, a catalog is a group of related fields.

Matching

___	**1.** =, <, >	a.	work surfaces
___	**2.** menus	b.	dot prompt
___	**3.** sideways	c.	pan
___	**4.** related files	d.	Control Center
___	**5.** DBMS	e.	quick report
___	**6.** important menu	f.	relational operators
___	**7.** selected records	g.	character, numeric
___	**8.** print the file	h.	query
___	**9.** enter direct command	i.	software
___	**10.** field types	j.	catalog

Test Answers

True/False

1. F	6. F	11. F	16. T
2. F	7. F	12. T	17. T
3. T	8. T	13. T	18. F
4. F	9. T	14. T	19. T
5. T	10. F	15. T	20. F

Matching

1. f
2. a
3. c
4. j
5. i
6. d
7. h
8. e
9. b
10. g

Close to Home

Databases are less "close to home" than word processing or spreadsheets. You are more likely to use databases in your work. However, some people do want to organize their home files so that they can be accessed in more than one way, and a database suits that purpose.

CHAPTER

12

Computer Graphics

Learning Objectives

- ❑ Appreciating the different types of graphics programs.
- ❑ Recognizing the variety of graphics input and output devices.
- ❑ Appreciating the various roles graphics are playing in business and other settings.

Why This Chapter Is Important

Computer-produced graphics are being used by people in diverse aspects of business. If you do not use them yourself, you will at least be seeing them in the business world. Furthermore, more and more people are turning to home-produced graphics for their own projects, whether or not in a business setting.

Mark Twain

William Shakespeare

Chapter Outline

The Rise of Computer Graphics

Early Computer Graphics

How Do Computers Create Graphics?
- Graphics Fundamentals
  - Bitmapped Graphics
  - Object Graphics
  - PostScript Graphics
- Graphics Input Devices
  - Light Pens
  - Game Sticks
  - Digitizers
  - Synthesizers
  - Scanners
  - Touch Screens
  - Digital Still Cameras
  - Digital Video Imaging
- Graphics Output Devices
  - Plotters
  - Printers
  - Overhead Transparencies
  - Overhead Devices
  - 35mm-Slide Makers
  - Video Cassette Recorders
  - CD-ROM
- Graphics Formats

Color Graphics

Using Computer Graphics
- Personal Graphics
- Business Graphics
- Illustration Graphics
- Mapping Graphics
- Video Graphics
- Multimedia
- CAD/CAM
- Games and Entertainment

A Graphics Future

Key Words

Algorithm ______________________________
____
____

Bitmapped graphics ______________________________
____
____

CAD/CAM ______________________________
____
____

Clip art ______________________________
____
____

Color model ______________________________
____
____

CGA ______________________________
____
____

Digital camera ______________________________
____
____

Digitizer ______________________________
____
____

Draw program ______________________________
____
____

Drum plotter ______________________________
____
____

EGA ______________________________
____
____

Flatbed plotter ______________________________
____
____

Fractal graphics ______________________________
____
____

Illustration graphics ______________________________
____
____

Joystick ______________________________
____
____

Light pen ______________________________
____
____

Mapping graphics ______________________________
____
____

Multimedia ______________________________
____
____

Object graphics ______________________________
____
____

Paint program ______________________________
____
____

Pixel ______________________________

Plotter ______________________________

Presentation graphics ______________________________

Raster graphics ______________________________

Resolution ______________________________

Scanner ______________________________

SVGA ______________________________

Swatch book ______________________________

Synthesizer ______________________________

Touch screen ______________________________

VGA ______________________________

Vector ______________________________

Video graphics ______________________________

XGA ______________________________

Study Hints

There is a great deal of detail in this chapter, which will be of great interest to those who have a serious interest in graphics. Those whose interest is more casual probably need not concern themselves with the minutia of hardware descriptions. Your best bet is to ask your instructor what level of detail is sufficient.

Self-Test

True/False

T F **1.** The greater the number of pixels, the poorer the screen clarity.

T F **2.** Touch screens are manipulated by using a finger.

T F **3.** Computer graphics are widely available for professional artists but not for the average computer user.

T F **4.** Clip art is only available on mainframe computers.

T F **5.** Bitmapped graphics use a series of lines.

T F **6.** A pixel is a picture element on the screen.

T F **7.** A pixel is a set of dots.

T F **8.** The better the screen's resolution, the better the clarity of the graphic produced.

T F **9.** Object graphics are created using a series of vectors.

T F **10.** Graphics programs that create object graphics are called draw programs.

T F **11.** Draw programs and paint programs use the same computer technique but different art forms.

T F **12.** Graphics software that use bitmapping techniques are called paint programs.

T F **13.** A synthesizer is used to produce music-related graphics.

T F **14.** A light pen has a special stylus to trace images.

T F **15.** Graphics formats determine the way a graphics image is stored on disk.

T F **16.** A flatbed plotter is a circular drum plotter.

T F **17.** Red-green-blue is the color model used on TV screens.

T F **18.** A swatch book is an array of colors produced on the screen.

T F **19.** Raster graphics is another name for bitmapped graphics.

T F **20.** Presentation graphics are usually used by home users for club newsletters.

Matching

___	**1.** predrawn images	a.	object graphics
___	**2.** mathematical formulas	b.	joy stick
___	**3.** picture element	c.	touch screen
___	**4.** raster graphics	d.	pixel
___	**5.** geometric shapes	e.	clip art
___	**6.** table-like	f.	scanner
___	**7.** clarity of detail	g.	flatbed plotter
___	**8.** games	h.	resolution
___	**9.** converts photographs	i.	fractals
___	**10.** finger input	j.	bitmapped

Test Answers

True/False

1. F	6. T	11. F	16. F
2. T	7. F	12. T	17. T
3. F	8. T	13. T	18. F
4. F	9. T	14. F	19. T
5. F	10. T	15. T	20. F

Matching

1. e	6. g
2. i	7. h
3. d	8. b
4. j	9. f
5. a	10. c

Close to Home

If you are artistic, but perhaps not an artist, you can express yourself on your personal computer by using art images created by others. All the non-exercise images in this book, for example, were created using clip art that can be purchased in any software store. Amateur artists use clip art to embellish their homegrown newsletters, reports, and even personal letters. Keep in mind that, although some software packages include their own clip art, clip art purchased separately is not self-sufficient software. Separate clip art images must imported directly into other software, probably word processing or desktop publishing software. Be certain that clip art you purchase separately works with the software you have.

For those who are artistically talented, there are several software packages that independently lend themselves to that talent. These software packages are often the same ones that professional graphics artist use. If you want to know what the professionals are using, check the credits for the graphics artworks in the main text.

Finally, if you are not particularly interested in creating anything of an artistic nature but would like to be an appreciative audience, you need look no further than your own TV screen. Many advertisements are completely produced by computer graphics software. In particular, pay attention to the pitches for the networks themselves; you can count on seeing their logos - the CBS "eye," for example - flashed on the screen in various graphic forms. In fact, just about anything that is not clearly film of human beings could be suspected of having computer origins.

CHAPTER

13

Computers on the Job: How Workers Use Computers

Learning Objectives

- ❑ Understand the variety of ways major organizations use computers.
- ❑ Appreciate the evolution of use of both large and small computers.
- ❑ Appreciate the impact of computers on the way workers do their jobs.

Why This Chapter Is Important

This chapter gives an overview of how computers are used on the job. This is particularly useful because most chapters focus on some specific aspect of computers.

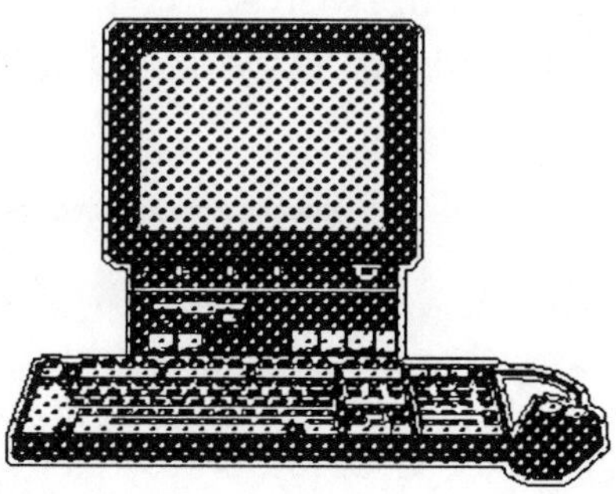

JUST THROW YOUR BODY ACROSS THE SCREEN

No, no. You need not go that far. But sometimes office workers get a little desperate when trying to protect typed screen data from the prying eyes of passersby. As often happens, technology side effects are mitigated by more technology - in this case, a filter that acts like a set of tiny venetian blinds. As you face the screen, it is perfectly clear. But a user to the side sees only a black screen.

Chapter Outline

Big Guys: Users of Large Computer Systems

Personal Computers in the Workplace
- Evolution of Personal Computer Use
- The Impact of Personal Computers
- Where PCs Are Almost a Job Requirement

How Computers Change the Way We Work
- The Name of the Game is Speed
- The Portable Worker
  - The Tools of Portability
  - The New Convenience

Software at Work
- Communications Software
- Graphics at Work
- Decision-making Software
- Storage and Retrieval Software
- Vertical Market Software

What Could Possibly Be Next?

Study Hints

This is an easy chapter, almost free from new concepts and buzzwords. Its purpose is to give you an overall picture of how computers are used by workers on the job.

MY FLYING OFFICE

Today's computer-conscious worker often thinks in terms of how to haul all the equipment along on a business trip. The idea is to do a little work, possibly using a laptop on the plane, and check in with the office when you reach your destination. But the airlines are taking that a step further: now you can plug right into the airplane's communication system, and send messages and data from your computer to the office while airborne. In fact, the airlines are in the process of turning each seat station into a full-service communications centers, including a display screen on the seatback in front of you. You can also receive messages and data from the office; incoming calls are wordlessly announced on the screen so as not to disturb snoozing passengers.

Self-Test

True/False

T F **1.** The companies that use mainframes today are mostly the same large corporations that were computer pioneers.

T F **2.** Early computer users used computers mostly for personal scheduling.

T F **3.** Computers are used in formal businesses offices but not in less formal settings such as sports or agriculture.

T F **4.** Many workers must know how to use personal computers to perform their jobs.

T F **5.** Vertical market software is used mostly by architects to plan high-rise buildings.

T F **6.** The major users of communications software are individuals using bulletin board systems.

T F **7.** Personal computer use in business has evolved in five stages, the highest use being an increase in individual worker productivity.

T F **8.** A key reason for the extensive use of personal computers in business is their low cost.

T F **9.** A key ingredient in worker portability is a laptop computer.

T F **10.** Many workers today need to know how to use computers as a component of their job.

Test Answers

True/False

1. T
2. F
3. F
4. T
5. F
6. F
7. F
8. T
9. T
10. T

CHAPTER

14

Management Information Systems: Managing Computer Resources

Learning Objectives

- ❑ Understanding the main functions of managers - planning, organizing, staffing, controlling, and directing.
- ❑ Knowledge of the purpose and components of a management information system (MIS).
- ❑ Understanding the functions of the personal computer manager.
- ❑ Understanding the need for decision support systems.

Why This Chapter Is Important

This is the most business-oriented chapter in the book. It provides a setting and an environment for computer uses in business. It also gives you some idea of what to expect from management when you enter business.

Chapter Outline

Key Words

Controlling

Decision support system (DSS)

Dependent variable

Detail report

Directing

Download

Exception report

Executive support system (ESS)

Groupware

Independent variable

Information center

Management information system (MIS)

MIS manager

Model

On-demand report

Organizing

Periodic report

Personal computer manager

Planning

Simulation

Staffing ______________________________
____
____

Summary report ______________________
____
____

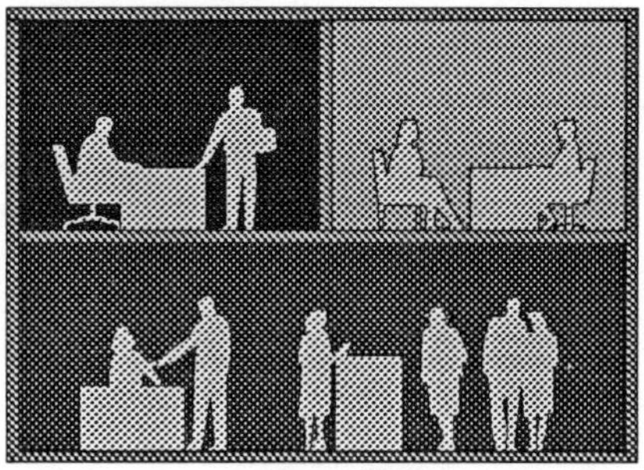

Study Hints

If you have business experience, the material on managers should seem to flow naturally, and you can relate it to what you already know. The material on management information systems (MIS) and decision support systems (DSS) is very fluid and can be seen changing with every new issue from the computing press.

Self-Test

True/False

T F **1.** The information center typically offers users training and assistance.

T F **2.** Periodic reports are offered on demand.

T F **3.** Downloading transfers files from a personal computer to a mainframe.

T F **4.** Decision support systems help managers in non-routine decision-making tasks.

T F **5.** A model is a mathematical representation of an artificial situation.

T F **6.** Middle-level managers focus on planning.

T F **7.** Inputs to a model are called independent variables.

T F **8.** Groupware is usually focused on groups of executives.

T F **9.** The use of personal computers by managers is declining.

T F **10.** Simulation is using a model to answer real-life situations.

Matching

___	1. model	a.	on-demand report
___	2. download	b.	exception report
___	3. executive support	c.	DSS
___	4. model inputs representation	d.	mathematical
___	5. unscheduled	e.	information center
___	6. unusual circumstances	f.	independent variables
___	7. totals or trends	g.	dependent variables
___	8. help users	h.	ESS
___	9. model outputs	i.	mainframe to micro
___	10. decision-making help	j.	summary report

Fill-In

1. What kind of software helps groups of office workers? 1. ____________________

2. Where can computer users go for help? 2. ____________________

3. What kind of reports show only data that reflects unusual circumstances? 3. ____________________

4. What are reports produced on a regular schedule called? 4. ____________________

5. What is the person in charge of personal computer acquisition and monitoring called? 5. ____________________

6. Which managers are primarily concerned with planning? 6. ____________________

7. What are the outputs of a model called? 7. ____________________

8. What is moving data from the mainframe to a personal computer called? 8. ____________________

9. What is a set of business systems designed to provide information for decision making called? 9. ____________________

10. List the five functions of management.
10.a. ____________________
b. ____________________
c. ____________________
d. ____________________
e. ____________________

Test Answers

True/False

1.	T	6.	F
2.	F	7.	T
3.	F	8.	F
4.	T	9.	F
5.	F	10.	T

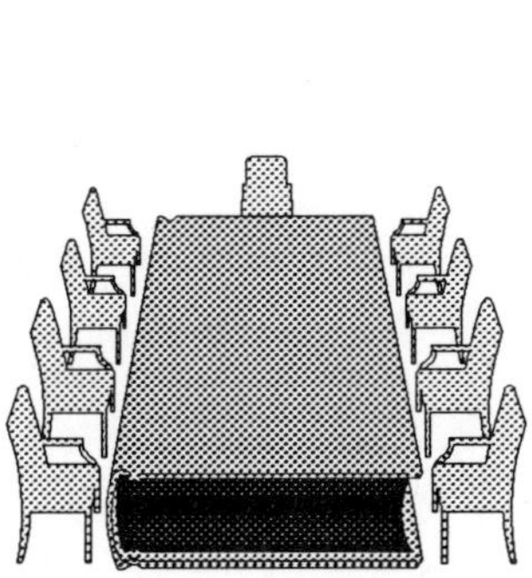

Matching

1.	d	6.	b
2.	i	7.	j
3.	h	8.	e
4.	f	9.	g
5.	a	10.	c

Fill-In

1. groupware
2. information center
3. exception report
4. periodic report
5. personal computer manager
6. top-level manager
7. dependent variable
8. downloading
9. management information system
10. a. planning
    b. organizing
    c. staffing
    d. controlling
    e. directing

Close to Home

This business-oriented chapter may not be "close to home" at all and may, in fact, not even be part of any business organization in your experience. Some of it is rather new, and some activities are limited mostly to large corporations.

CHAPTER

15

Security, Privacy, and Ethics: Protecting Hardware, Software, and Data

Learning Objectives

- ❑ Awareness of the problem of computer crime, including criminal profiles, types of crimes, and the difficulties of discovery and prosecution.
- ❑ Awareness of the need for security, including disaster recovery plans, software and data security, and security legislation.
- ❑ Understanding the importance of privacy and how it is affected by the computer age.
- ❑ Understanding the importance of ethics as related to a computer environment.

Why This Chapter Is Important

Few issues are as totally pervasive in our society as security and privacy; we feel it is our birthright to keep ourselves and our possessions safe and free from prying eyes. Yet the computer, the instrument that has represented so much of what is good in our society, can also be used to undermine our security and privacy. This chapter contains information of value to anyone musing on the impact of the computer on people's lives.

OWN A CAR? YOUR PRIVACY MAY BE IN DANGER

In approximately half the states it is perfectly legal obtain the names and addresses of car owners. Some states go even further, selling the information wholesale on computer tapes to all comers, from insurance companies to marketers to detectives. Furthermore, anyone can jot down a license plate number and go the motor vehicles department to get the person's name and address. California, spurred by privacy invasions by crazed movie fans, recently passed a law to keep such information private.

Chapter Outline

Computer Crime
- Who Is the Computer Criminal?
- Types and Methods of Computer Crime
- Discovery and Prosecution

Security: Playing It Safe
- Identification and Access: Who Goes There?
- When Disaster Strikes: What Do You Have to Lose
- Disaster Recovery Plan
- Software Security
- Data Security
- Secured Waste
- Passwords
- Internal Controls
- Auditor Checks
  - Cryptography
  - Applicant Screening
  - Separation of Employee Functions
  - Built-In Software Protection
- Security Considerations for Personal Computers
- Viruses and Vaccines
  - Transmitting a Virus
  - Damage from Viruses
  - Prevention

Privacy: Keeping Personal Information Personal

A Matter of Ethics

Copying Software
- OK If I Copy That Software?
- Why Those Extra Copies?
- Site Licensing
- Know Your Legal Rights (and Wrongs)

Paying Attention Because We Must

Key Words

Biometrics ______________________
____
____

Bomb ____________________________
____
____

Cold site ________________________
____
____

Computer Fraud and Abuse Act ______
____
____

Consortium _______________________
____
____

Copy protection ___________________
____
____

Copyrighted software _______________
____
____

Cryptography _____________________
____
____

Data diddling ______________________
____
____

Data Encryption Standard (DES) ____
____
____

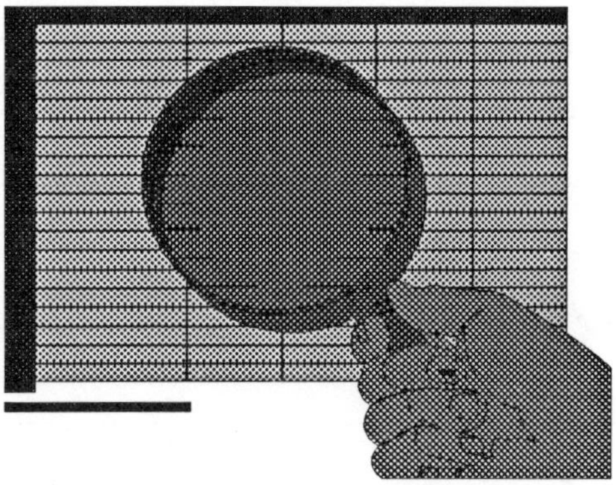

THE TALE TAXES TELL

Perhaps you have heard of personal computer software to keep track of income taxes. It's a bit of a nuisance, keying in all those receipts, but the payoff at tax time is gratifying: No rummaging through shoeboxes full of tiny papers, no stacking and sorting on the dining room table. Your computer gives you orderly printouts, according to the kinds of expenses represented. These records also are a fine tool to have at the ready if you are audited.

But wait. What else could be done with those files? Some people use their home computers to enter income tax data directly to the IRS. This becomes a privacy issue. Suppose, for example, that same data was arranged not by type of expense but by date. As you scroll through the data it would be pretty easy to identify the times you went out, where you stayed, restaurants where you ate, phone calls placed, books purchased, and so forth. A virtual diary - devastatingly revealing - comes into focus. What other use might be made of that data? This is the kind of thing privacy advocates have been warning about for years. We are not there yet, not even close, but it is food for thought.

Data leakage ____________________

Disaster recovery plan ____________________

Encryption ____________________

Fair Credit Reporting Act ____________________

Federal Privacy Act ____________________

Freedom of Information Act ____________________

Hacker ____________________

Hot site ____________________

Logic bomb ____________________

Password ____________________

Piggybacking ____________________

Piracy ____________________

Privacy ____________________

Public domain ____________________

Salami technique ____________________

Scavenging ____________________

Security ____________________

Shareware ____________________

Site license ____________________

Software piracy ____________________

Surge protector ____________________

Trap door ____________________

Trojan Horse ____________________
____
____

Vaccine ________________________
____
____

Video Privacy Protection Act _______
____
____

Virus __________________________
____
____

Worm___________________________
____
____

Zapping_________________________
____
____

COMPUTERIZED LOCKS

Who wins, the people who make the locks or the people who crack them? The battle that has raged for years is now tilting to the lock makers, who are relying on computer technology to make a foolproof lock. The lock, powered by a microprocessor inside, has a liquid crystal display to show the correct code numbers as they are input. So far, the locks are impervious to outside assault, including using other computers.

Study Hints

The information on computer crime is relatively easy to study, but the material on security and privacy is more complex. Separate the security issues by hardware, software, and data. Consider the impact of security issues on both the organization and the individual. Pay particular attention to the legislation.

Self-Test

Multiple Choice

1. A computer crime in which money is embezzled in small amounts over time is
   a. the salami method
   b. blue-collar crime
   c. the Trojan Horse
   d. data diddling

2. To protect data from being stolen, an organization must plan
   a. a hot site
   b. a recovery plan
   c. a cold site
   d. data security

3. One safeguard against theft or alteration of data is the use of
   a. DES
   b. the Trojan Horse
   c. identical passwords
   d. data diddling

4. The legislation that prohibits government agencies and contractors from keeping secret personal files on individuals
   a. was not passed
   b. passed in 1974
   c. is the Freedom Act
   d. passed in 1970

5. A student who managed to modify her grades before they were entered into the computer file could be said to be
   a. piggybacking
   b. data diddling
   c. using the salami method
   d. altering stored data

6. Computer crimes are usually
   a. easy to detect
   b. blue-collar crimes
   c. prosecuted
   d. discovered accidentally

7. The "what you are" criterion for computer system access involves
   a. a badge
   b. a password
   c. biometrics
   d. a magnetized card

8. The key factor in a computer installation that has met with disaster is the
   a. equipment replacement
   b. insurance coverage
   c. loss of hardware
   d. loss of processing ability

9. In anticipation of physical destruction, every computer organization should have a
   - a. biometric scheme
   - b. cold site
   - c. disaster recovery plan
   - d. hot site

10. Software piracy includes
    - a. badge theft
    - b. program duplication
    - c. copyrighting
    - d. data alteration

11. Authorization to make multiple software copies is called
    - a. piggybacking
    - b. scavenging
    - c. site licensing
    - d. copy protection

12. Secured waste and cryptography are two steps toward
    - a. data security
    - b. data theft
    - c. built-in software protection
    - d. piracy detection

13. The weakest link in any computer system is the
    - a. people in it
    - b. password
    - c. hardware
    - d. software

14. A device that prevents electrical problems from affecting data files:
    - a. site license
    - b. hot site
    - c. Trojan Horse
    - d. surge protector

15. One form of built-in software protection for data is
    - a. secured waste
    - b. user profile
    - c. applicant screening
    - d. auditor checks

16. The law that prohibits government agencies and contractors from keeping secret personal files on individuals
    - a. was passed in 1970
    - b. was never passed
    - c. is the Federal Privacy Act
    - d. is the Freedom of Information Act

17. Empty shells in which a company may install its own computer are called
    - a. restoration sites
    - b. hot sites
    - c. cold sites
    - d. hardware sites

18. A program written when the programmer is employed by an organization is owned by
    - a. the programmer
    - b. the state
    - c. no one
    - d. the organization

19. Security protection for personal computers includes
a. internal components
b. software
c. locks and cables
d. all of these

20. The secret words or numbers to be typed in on a keyboard before any activity can take place are called
a. biometric data
b. passwords
c. data encryptions
d. private words

21. Another name for an antivirus is
a. vaccine
b. trojan horse
c. worm
d. DES

22. Another name for free software:
a. encrypted
b. public domain
c. copy protected
d. shareware

23. A virus that replicates itself is called a:
a. bug
b. vaccine
c. worm
d. bomb

24. A program whose sabotage depends on certain conditions is called a:
a. bug
b. vaccine
c. worm
d. bomb

25. A person who gains illegal access to a computer system:
a. hacker
b. software pirate
c. worm
d. zapper

True/False

T F 1. Most computer organizations cannot afford consortiums.

T F 2. A profile of a computer criminal suggests that he or she is likely to be regarded as an ideal employee.

T F 3. The Trojan Horse is an embezzling technique.

T F 4. If a computer crime is detected, prosecution is assured.

T F 5. Computer security is achieved by physically restricting access.

T F **6.** Fingerprints are an example of biometrics.

T F **7.** The actual loss of hardware is the major security problem due to its expense.

T F **8.** A disaster recovery plan is a scheme devised in anticipation of major software piracy.

T F **9.** It is legitimate to make a copy of software for backup purposes.

T F **10.** Passwords, auditor checks, and cryptography are data protection techniques.

T F **11.** The science of studying individual body characteristics is called biometrics.

T F **12.** Passwords are best changed annually.

T F **13.** The Federal Privacy Act of 1974 was the first legislation relating to privacy.

T F **14.** Data diddling is a criminal method whereby data is modified before it goes into a computer file.

T F **15.** Unauthorized manipulation of programs falls into one of the three categories of computer crime.

T F **16.** A mutual aid pact with another computer facility is one possibility for a disaster recovery plan.

T F **17.** A key element of a disaster recovery plan is to establish priorities, that is, which programs must be up and running first.

T F **18.** The Data Encryption Standard is a standardized list of passwords for software security.

T F **19.** By allowing a programmer also to be a computer operator, a computer organization can improve security.

T F **20.** Software can be patented.

Matching

___	1. altered program	a.	biometrics
___	2. what they know	b.	data diddling
___	3. Freedom of Information Act	c.	disaster recovery plan
___	4. what they are	d.	public domain
___	5. DES	e.	system of safeguards
___	6. modified data	f.	passwords
___	7. The Copyright Act	g.	1976
___	8. cold sites	h.	1970
___	9. free software	i.	Trojan Horse
___	10. security	j.	standardized public key

Fill-In

1. What is an environmentally-suitable empty shell into which a computer organization can put its computer system? 1. ________________

2. What is a system of safeguards to protect a computer system and data from damage or unauthorized access called? 2. ________________

3. What is bypassing security systems with an illicitly acquired software package called? 3. ________________

4. What field is concerned with the measurement of individual body characteristics? 4. ________________

5. What is the name for a fully equipped computer center to be used in the event of a disaster? **5.** ____________

6. What is the assurance to individuals that personal property is used properly called? **6.** ____________

7. What is a person who gains access to a computer system illegally called? **7.** ____________

8. Name a standardized public key by which senders and receivers can scramble and unscramble their messages. **8.** ____________

9. What are the four categories of authorized access to a computer system?

9.a. ____________

b. ____________

c. ____________

d. ____________

10. What is a term for the unauthorized copying of software? **10.** ____________

11. What law, passed in 1970, allows ordinary citizens to have access to data gathered by federal agencies? **11.** ____________

12. Which law prohibits government agencies and private contractors hired by the government from keeping secret personal files? **12.** ____________

13. The Fair Credit Reporting Act of 1970 gives people access to what information? **13.** ____________

14. Software that is freely given away but with the hope of a contribution is called: **14.** ____________

15. Does a program belong to the programmer or the employing organization? **15.** ____________

16. Which is potentially the least damaging type of security violation: hardware, software, or data? **16.** ____________

17. What type of technique is the salami method? **17.** ____________

18. What is placing an illicit program within a completed program, allowing unauthorized entry called? **18.** ____________

19. What is a permit to make multiple copies of software called? **19.** ____________

20. List the three general categories of computer crime. **20.a.** ____________

b. ____________

c. ____________

SIGNATURE RECOGNITION

Technology is available today to learn what your signature looks like and how you write it. Your signature can be analyzed through pen pressure, character shape, and pen acceleration. With each signature, the computer updates your record to allow for natural changes in your signature over time.

Test Answers

Multiple Choice

1. a	6. d	11. c	16. c	21. a
2. d	7. c	12. a	17. c	22. b
3. a	8. d	13. a	18. d	23. c
4. b	9. c	14. d	19. d	24. d
5. b	10. b	15. b	20. b	25. a

True/False

1. T	6. T	11. T	16. T
2. T	7. F	12. F	17. T
3. F	8. F	13. F	18. F
4. F	9. T	14. T	19. F
5. F	10. T	15. T	20. T

Matching

1. i	6. b
2. f	7. g
3. h	8. c
4. a	9. d
5. j	10. e

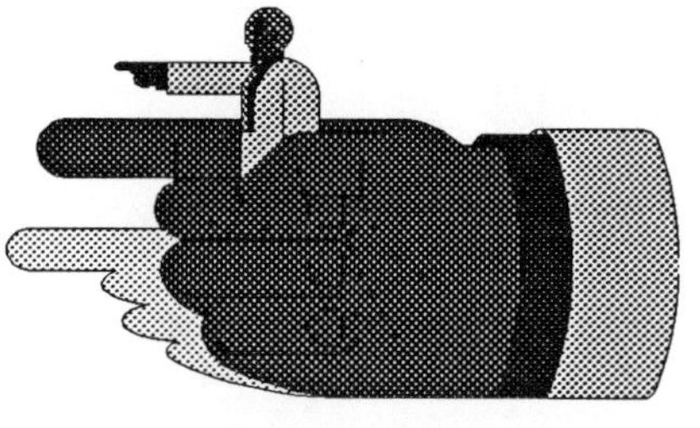

WHYS AND WHATS FOR HACKERS

A group of five New York teenage hackers were happy to announce *why* they broke into computer systems. Top on the list was to impress their friends, followed by harassing people they didn't like, getting computer services without paying, and getting information they could sell. Prosecutors responded with the *what* - charges of computer tampering, computer fraud, wire fraud, wiretapping, and conspiracy.

Fill-In

1. cold site
2. security
3. zapping
4. biometrics
5. hot site
6. privacy
7. hacker
8. Data Encryption Standard (DES)
9. a. what you have
   b. what you know
   c. what you do
   d. what you are
10. software piracy
11. Freedom of Information
12. Federal Privacy Act
13. credit reports
14. shareware
15. the organization
16. hardware
17. embezzlement
18. trap door
19. site license
20. a. theft of computer time
    b. theft or damage to programs/data
    c. alteration of computer

Close to Home

This chapter should touch you personally. If you tend to be a worrier, this chapter should add new furrows to your brow: There *are* some serious issues here. Most security-related discussions focus on students and employees illegally accessing, and perhaps manipulating, data. But the imagination can run far afield: What about infiltration of computer systems by organized crime? What about access by foreign, unfriendly governments? What about the possibility of our own government spying on us, Big Brother style? These scenarios are chilling, but all are possible with the technology that exists today.

CHAPTER

16

Modern Trends: Artificial Intelligence, Expert Systems, Robotics

Learning Objectives

- ❑ Familiarity with the concepts and terms of artificial intelligence, expert systems, and robotics.
- ❑ Understanding how these fields of study have developed.
- ❑ Understanding the impact of these fields on business and every day life.

Why This Chapter Is Important

It is always important to give at least a cursory look to the most futuristic aspect of any field of study. This chapter is necessarily light, but it paints a broad picture of what computers could become in the not-so-distant future.

THINKING SOFTWARE

Real-life thinking software:

- Human services: Decide if applicant receives welfare.
- IRS: Read tax returns and spot fraud.
- Marketing: Uncover likely buyers for new products.
- Communications: Diagnose customer phone problems.
- Transportation: Schedule routine airplane maintenance.
- Finance: Predict stock performance.

Chapter Outline

The Artificial Intelligence Field
- Early Mishaps
- How Computers Learn
- The Artificial Intelligence Debate
- Brainpower: Neural networks
- The Famous Turing Test

The Natural Language Factor

Fuzzy Logic

Expert Systems
- Expert Systems in Business
- Building an Expert System
- The Outlook for Expert Systems

Robotics
- Robots in the Factory
- Robot Vision
- Field Robots

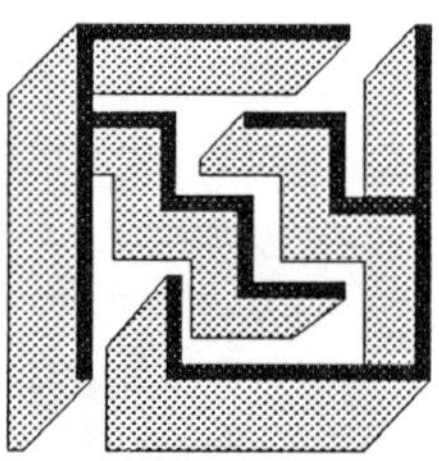

Study Hints

No hints here. Just enjoy. If you have a greater interest, look for magazines on artificial intelligence in your school library.

McDonald's restaurants, already noted for their speedy service, are cranking efficiency up another notch. Their French fries and soft drinks will be made by robots. McDonald's calls the new team players ARCH, for Automated Robotic Crew Helper.

As a maker of French fries, Archie moves the baskets around for filling, cooking, and emptying, and even shakes the basket during frying. Archie uses optical sensors as "eyes" to alert the computer to problems such as an empty or overloaded basket.

For drink-making duty, Archie responds to the push of a cash machine button by a human crew member. Archie puts the correct amount of ice in a cup and moves it under the right spigot. After the cup is filled, it is moved by conveyor belt to a location where human crew can pick it up and pass it on to the customer.

Archie, by the way, bears no resemblance to the cute humanoid robot shown here. He's just a machine.

Key Words

Artificial intelligence ______________

Expert shell ______________

Expert system ______________

Field robot ______________

Inference engine ______________

Knowledge base ______________

Knowledge engineer ______________

Natural language ______________

Neural network ______________

Robot ______________

Turing test ______________

Vision robot ______________

SMARTHOUSE

Some people call it robohouse, but, since you have control, *smarthouse* is probably a better name. With computer controls in place, you can: call as you are leaving work to start the prepared dinner cooking; program the dishwasher to turn on at midnight when electricity rates are lower; program the window shades to raise and lower, and lights to come on and off randomly, while you are away on vacation; automatically control security, temperature, humidity, air quality, and much, much more.

Self-Test

True/False

T F **1.** Artificial intelligence has enjoyed wide respect from scientists and the government from its inception.

T F **2.** Artificial intelligence is an umbrella term to cover many subjects.

T F **3.** A knowledge base is a set of facts and rules about those facts.

T F **4.** Fuzzy logic tends to mimic exact computer logic.

T F **5.** Early attempts to translate human language failed.

T F **6.** An expert system is a kind of software.

T F **7.** An expert shell is used by the end users of the expert system.

T F **8.** Vision robots have sight capability that is significantly less than human capability.

T F **9.** Field robots can do many tasks that are undesirable for humans.

T F **10.** A knowledge engineer is a customer who uses an expert system.

T F **11.** Dumb terminals can process, but not store, data.

T F **12.** Most organization who want an expert system do not attempt to build it from scratch.

T F **13.** Using computers to mimic natural language is a relatively easy task for computer experts.

T F **14.** Neural networks are chips designed to mimic the human brain.

T F **15.** Computers generally solve problems in a step-by-step fashion.

T F **16.** People generally solve problems in a step-by-step fashion.

T F **17.** An underlying assumption of artificial intelligence is that the computer can learn.

T F **18.** The medical and scientific communities were early users of expert systems.

T F **19.** An inference engine is the same thing as a knowledge base.

T F **20.** Understanding natural language is a skill thought to require intelligence.

T F **21.** At one time, AI scientists were the subject of ridicule.

T F **22.** In general, a given word in a natural language has a single meaning.

T F **23.** The Turing test proved conclusively that computers could match human brainpower.

T F **24.** Most computer chess games can still be beaten by average human chess players.

T F **25.** Most robots today are used in scientific experiments.

Matching

___	**1.** robot	a. AI test
___	**2.** Turing	b. vision robot
___	**3.** natural language	c. works with human expert
___	**4.** expert shell	d. field robot
___	**5.** recognizes objects	e. interprets rules
___	**6.** neural network	f. software
___	**7.** inspects nuclear plant	g. computer controlled
___	**8.** knowledge engineer	h. human speech
___	**9.** set of facts, rules	i. mimics the brain
___	**10.** inference engine	j. knowledge base

Fill-In

1. The generic term for using computers for jobs requiring human characteristics: 1. ______________

2. What is the term for software that can be to build an expert system? 2. ______________

3. What is the software that interprets facts and rules? 3. ______________

4. What kind of robot can perform inspections and other dangerous tasks? 4. ______________

5. The person who extract information from the human expert is called: 5. ______________

6. Computers whose chips mimic the human brain are called: 6. ______________

7. A device that can physically manipulate its surroundings is called: 7. ______________

8. A set of facts and a set of rules about those facts is called: 8. ______________

9. The language used by humans is called: 9. ______________

10. What kind of root can distinguish objects by their shape or color? 10. ______________

Test Answers

True/False

1. F	6. T	11. T	16. F	21. T
2. T	7. F	12. T	17. T	22. F
3. T	8. T	13. F	18. T	23. F
4. F	9. T	14. T	19. F	24. F
5. T	10. F	15. T	20. T	25. F

Matching

1. g
2. a
3. h
4. f
5. b
6. i
7. d
8. c
9. j
10. e

Fill-In

1. artificial intelligence
2. expert shell
3. inference engine
4. field robot
5. knowledge engineer
6. neural network
7. robot
8. knowledge base
9. natural language
10. vision robot

Close to Home

It may seem that, since you do not have a robot as a member of your household, this subject matter does not hit very close to home. In fact, the closest you will get to the subject matter in this chapter may be some customer-related expert system. But all that could change in the not-so-distant future. Futurists often hammer on the theme of the computer-controlled domestic servant. Robots are already in place in the homes of some handicapped individuals. The possibilities of more general use are not far-fetched.

APPENDIX

A

The Programming Process

Learning Objectives

- ❑ Understanding fundamental flowcharting techniques and pseudocode.
- ❑ Introduction to the control structures of structured programming.
- ❑ Understand the rationale for structured programming and its basic concepts.

Why This Chapter Is Important

Those who plan a career in the computer field, even in such peripheral areas as sales, will be distinctly handicapped if they do not understand the rudiments of programming. This chapter also provides the rationale and foundation for the current use of structured techniques.

Chapter Outline

Planning the Solution

Flowcharts

Structure Charts

Pseudocode

Structured Programming
- Sequence
- Selection
- Iteration

Using Flowcharts, Structure Charts, and Pseudocode

Programmers Emerge
- Early Programming
- Structured Programming Takes Off
- Expanding the Structured Programming Concept
- Modularity
- Is There a Future for Structured Programming?

A Career in Programming?

Key Words

Branch ______

Cohesion ______

Coupling ______

Compare operation ______

Connector symbol ______

Control structure ______

Decision box ______

DOUNTIL ______

DOWHILE ______

Edsger Dijkstra ______

End of file ______

Entry point ______

Exit point ______

Flowchart ______

Hierarchy chart ______

IF-THEN-ELSE ______

Initialize ______

Input/output box ______

Iteration ______

Leading decision ______

Loop ______

Module ______

Priming read ______

Process box ______

Pseudocode ______

Selection ______

Sequence ______

Single entry ______

Single exit ______

Start/stop symbol ______

Structure chart ______

Structured programming ______

Top-down design ______

Trailing decision ______

Study Hints

The material in this chapter may be difficult at first. Even if you have a little experience with programming, you are probably making some adjustments to a structured style. Study and restudy the text examples carefully.

Self-Test

Multiple Choice

1. In flowcharting, actions to be taken are represented by a(n)
   a. process symbol
   b. oval symbol
   c. decision symbol
   d. diamond symbol

2. To set the starting values of storage locations is to
   a. compare
   b. loop
   c. initialize
   d. iterate

3. Sequence, selection, and iteration are
   a. control structures
   b. IF-THEN statements
   c. comparison operations
   d. unlimited structures

4. If the decision on when to stop repeating is placed at the end of all the loop statements, the loop is a(n)
   a. IF-THEN
   b. DOUNTIL
   c. DOWHILE
   d. SEQUENCE

5. After stating the solution to a problem in pseudocode, the next step in development would be
   a. testing the program
   b. documenting the program
   c. coding the program
   d. translating the program

6. The ANSI symbol for a connector in flowcharting is a(n)
   a. rectangle
   b. diamond
   c. oval
   d. circle

7. The read statement before a loop begins is sometimes called the
   a. priming read
   b. beginning read
   c. first read
   d. initial read

8. The diamond-shaped box with two paths, or branches is a
   a. start/stop symbol
   b. decision symbol
   c. process symbol
   d. connector symbol

9. The man who wrote the famous letter about GOTOs being harmful is
   a. Turner
   b. Dijkstra
   c. Bohm
   d. Jacopini

10. "Spaghetti code" is a reference to
- **a.** a system
- **b.** GOTOs
- **c.** pseudocode
- **d.** a module

11. A set of logically related program statements is called
- **a.** a system
- **b.** a module
- **c.** pseudocode
- **d.** a programming team

12. The measure of the strength of the relationship between two modules is called
- **a.** cohesion
- **b.** dependence
- **c.** control
- **d.** coupling

13. Reducing the number of GOTOs reduces the number of
- **a.** modules
- **b.** selections
- **c.** programming errors
- **d.** iterations

14. A module should have
- **a.** weak cohesion
- **b.** multi-entry/single exit
- **c.** a double function
- **d.** weak coupling

15. Charting and pseudocode are part of which programming phase:
- **a.** documenting
- **b.** testing
- **c.** planning
- **d.** coding

True/False

T F **1.** An advantage of pseudocode is that it can be used to plan and execute a program.

T F **2.** Process boxes in flowcharting have two exits called paths.

T F **3.** A decision box contains a compare operation.

T F **4.** Structured programming emphasizes breaking a program into logical sections.

T F **5.** Three basic control structures are input, process, and output.

T F **6.** DOWHILE and DOUNTIL are examples of a selection pattern.

T F **7.** When looping, the decision on when to stop repeating must be placed at the end of all loop statements.

T F 8. IF-THEN is an example of an iteration control structure.

T F 9. For every flowchart decision box, there must be a connector box.

T F 10. An iteration is the repetition of instructions under certain conditions.

T F 11. A single page of coded program instructions is often considered an ideal module size.

T F 12. The cohesion of modules should be weak to make future changes in program structure easier.

T F 13. A structure chart graphically describes program functions from the general level to the detailed level.

T F 14. Top-down design is one aspect of structured design.

T F 15. Structured programming increases program clarity and readability.

Matching

___	1. structure chart	a. limited structures
___	2. coupling	b. procedural language
___	3. top-down design	c. Jacopini
___	4. structured programming	d. inner strength
___	5. GOTO	e. hierarchy chart
___	6. cohesion	f. just one
___	7. a control structure	g. spaghetti code
___	8. step-by-step process	h. should be weak
___	9. module entry	i. identify major functions
___	10. Bohm	j. sequence

Test Answers

Multiple Choice

1. a	6. d	11. b
2. c	7. a	12. d
3. a	8. b	13. c
4. b	9. b	14. d
5. c	10. b	15. c

True/False

1. F	6. F	11. T
2. F	7. F	12. F
3. T	8. F	13. F
4. T	9. T	14. T
5. F	10. T	15. T

Matching

1. e	6. d
2. h	7. j
3. i	8. b
4. a	9. f
5. g	10. c

Close to Home

If you are contemplating a career as a computer programmer, this chapter is, of course, of vital interest to you. From this foundation you can move on to the use of a programming language and actually plan and develop computer programs.

APPENDIX

B

History and Industry: The Continuing Story of the Computer Age

Learning Objectives

- ❑ Understanding the story of how computer technology unfolded, with particular emphasis on the "generations."
- ❑ Understanding how people and events affected the development of computers.
- ❑ Familiarity with the story of microcomputer development.
- ❑ Acquaintance with the development of software.

Why This Chapter Is Important

If you are truly interested in a field of study, it is important to have some understanding of its history. The computer field, perhaps more than any other, has made an extraordinary impact in a very short time period, and most of that time was during recent years.

Those of us who were in the industry then - and therefore should have known what was going on - often failed to perceive the enormity of the events around us. Like so many others, we were just moving through our lives, earning a living, and doing what was expected of us. Yes, computers were interesting, but it became tiresome trying to explain to people what we really "did" for a living. We never dreamed it would come to this.

Now the Computer Revolution is truly here in full force. The impact it is having on society cannot be missed by anyone who has eyes to see. You who are just beginning your computer careers can place yourself squarely on a time line in the midst of the revolution. You have become aware of the people and machines that have gone before you, and you will be prepared for the wonders still to come.

Chapter Outline

Babbage and the Countess

Herman Hollerith: The Census Has Never Been the Same

Watson of IBM: Ornery but Rather Successful

The Start of the Modern Era

The Computer Age Begins
- The First Generation, 1951-1958: The Vacuum Tube
- The Second Generation, 1959-1964: The Transistor
- The Third Generation, 1965-1970: The Integrated Circuit
- The Fourth Generation, 1971-Present: The Microprocessor
- The Fifth Generation: Japan's Challenge

The Special Story of Petsonal Computers
- I Built It in My Garage
- The IBM PC Phenomenon
- The Story Continues

Key Words

Analytical engine ____________________
____
____

Assembly language ____________________
____
____

John Atanasoff ____________________
____
____

Atanasoff-Berry Computer (ABC) ___
____
____

Charles Babbage ____________________
____
____

Clifford Berry ____________________
____
____

Difference engine ____________________
____
____

J. Presper Eckert ____________________
____
____

ENIAC ____________________________
____
____

High-level language ____________________________
____
____

Herman Hollerith ____________________________
____
____

Steve Jobs ____________________________
____
____

Integrated circuit ____________________________
____
____

Ada Lovelace ____________________________
____
____

Magnetic core ____________________________
____
____

Mark I ____________________________
____
____

John Mauchly ____________________________
____
____

Microprocessor ____________________________
____
____

MITS Altair ____________________________
____
____

Semiconductor ____________________________
____
____

Silicon chip ____________________________
____
____

Symbolic language ____________________________
____
____

Tabulating machine ____________________________
____
____

Transistor ____________________________
____
____

UNIVAC I ____________________________
____
____

Vacuum tube ____________________________
____
____

Thomas J. Watson ____________________________
____
____

Steve Wozniak ____________________________
____
____

Study Hints

Begin by making a careful association of people with machines: Babbage with the difference engine, and so forth. There are quite a number of such associations, so you might like to make a separate list as a study guide.

The most important part of the chapter, and the part that should command your greatest attention, is the information on generations. Even though people like Babbage made significant contributions, the spectacular development of computers as we know them today is to be found in the computer generations of recent decades.

Self-Test

Multiple Choice

1. Charles Babbage invented the
   a. Mark I
   b. abacus
   c. difference engine
   d. adding machine

2. The analytical engine used
   a. a punched card system
   b. electrical power
   c. vacuum tubes
   d. magnetic tape

3. The first computer to use electrical power was developed by
   a. Herman Hollerith
   b. John V. Atanasoff
   c. Thomas J. Watson
   d. Howard Aiken

4. The Mark I was built by
   a. Thomas Watson
   b. John V. Atanasoff
   c. Dr. John Mauchly
   d. Howard Aiken

5. The first digital computer to work electronically was the
   a. UNIVAC
   b. Mark I
   c. Atanasoff-Berry Computer
   d. analytical machine

6. The ENIAC, using ABC principles, was designed by
   a. Charles Babbage
   b. John V. Atanasoff
   c. Bell Laboratories
   d. Mauchly and Eckert

7. Hollerith's Tabulating Machine Company eventually became
   a. IBM
   b. Apple
   c. AT&T
   d. General Electric

8. First-generation computers were characterized by the use of the
   a. microprocessor
   b. transistor
   c. vacuum tube
   d. integrated circuit

9. Primary storage for the UNIVAC was via
   a. punched cards
   b. magnetic cores
   c. transistors
   d. disk packs

10. Transistors characterized a major improvement over
   a. semiconductors
   b. vacuum tubes
   c. disk packs
   d. the integrated circuit

11. Assembly languages, or symbolic languages, use
   a. binary code
   b. numbers
   c. abbreviations for instructions
   d. English words

12. COBOL and FORTRAN are examples of
   a. machine languages
   b. assembly languages
   c. higher-level languages
   d. obsolete languages

13. Silicon chips of integrated circuits (ICs) marked the advent of the
   a. second generation
   b. third generation
   c. fourth generation
   d. fifth generation

14. IBM's System/360 family of computers was introduced during the
   a. 1950s
   b. second generation
   c. third generation
   d. 1970s

15. The fourth generation is identified by the
   a. minicomputer
   b. IBM System/360
   c. introduction of ICs
   d. microprocessor

16. The first Apple computer was built in
   a. a garage
   b. an apartment
   c. a warehouse
   d. a factory

17. IBM PC look-alikes were called
   a. PC XTs
   b. clones
   c. emulators
   d. identicals

18. The general-purpose processor-on-a-chip is otherwise known as the
   a. ENIAC
   b. pocket calculator
   c. microcomputer
   d. microprocessor

19. A 10-year project to develop a fifth generation was initiated by
    a. Germany
    b. USA
    c. France
    d. Japan

20. Some IBM PC versions
    a. XT, RT, PCjr
    b. AT, RT, TT
    c. AT, BT, PCjr
    d. AT, BT, CT

True/False

T F 1. The analytical engine embodied the five key concepts of a computer system.

T F 2. Countess Ada Lovelace could be considered the first computer programmer.

T F 3. Hollerith's tabulating machine was driven by mechanical power.

T F 4. Thomas G. Watson, Sr., developed the Mark I, an electromechanical computer.

T F 5. The ABC was built by Howard Aiken and Clifford Berry.

T F 6. The ENIAC had a large storage capacity and was a very flexible system.

T F 7. The ENIAC, made operational in 1946, was the world's first electronic digital computer.

T F 8. Thomas Watson was a dominating force at IBM.

T F 9. Charles Babbage and Ada Lovelace worked together to produce the ENIAC.

T F 10. The first generation, characterized by the vacuum tube, encompassed all computer development prior to 1960.

T F 11. The UNIVAC used thousands of vacuum tubes.

T F 12. A drawback of vacuum tubes was temperature control.

T F 13. Magnetic core was the dominant form of primary storage technology for two decades.

T F 14. The transistor of the second generation was faster and more reliable than the vacuum tube but used more energy.

T F 15. Both assembly languages and higher-level languages were developed during the second generation.

T F 16. The first higher-level language to receive widespread acceptance was COBOL.

T F 17. In 1962 the first removable disk pack was marketed, enabling users to have fast access to desired data.

T F 18. Integrated circuits, ICs, marked the advent of the third generation.

T F 19. Microprocessors led to the development of the microcomputer.

T F 20. The Altair was developed by John Atanasoff.

Matching

___	1. Howard Aiken	a. assembly language
___	2. third generation	b. Mark I
___	3. formula translator	c. magnetic core
___	4. Thomas Watson	d. ENIAC
___	5. symbolic language	e. transistor
___	6. Bell Laboratories	f. vacuum tubes
___	7. Herman Hollerith	g. IBM
___	8. John Mauchly	h. tabulating machine
___	9. UNIVAC	i. integrated circuit
___	10. primary storage	j. FORTRAN

Fill-In

1. What were the five key concepts of modern computers embodied in Charles Babbage's analytical engine?

   1.a. ____________________

   b. ____________________

   c. ____________________

   d. ____________________

   e. ____________________

2. The technology of the second generation:

   2. ____________________

3. Who is considered the world's first computer programmer? Whom did this person assist?

   3.a. ____________________

   b. ____________________

4. Who built IBM into a dominant force in the business machine market?

   4. ____________________

5. What machine was used in the U.S. Census of 1890?

   5. ____________________

6. Who were the two men to devise the first electronic digital computer? What did they call their machine?

   6.a. ____________________

   b. ____________________

   c. ____________________

7. To whom did Watson give research funds to build an electromechanical computer? What machine resulted from this funding?

   7.a. ____________________

   b. ____________________

8. What was the world's first general-purpose electronic digital computer? When was it made operational?

8.a. ______________________

b. ______________________

9. The first commercial computer, delivered in 1951:

9. ______________________

10. What are the technological developments that mark the first, second, third, and fourth generations of the computer age?

10.a. ______________________

b. ______________________

c. ______________________

d. ______________________

11. What was the principal form of technology used for primary storage for the first two decades of the computer age?

11. ______________________

12. What was introduced in 1957 as a faster, more compact method than punched cards and as a supplement to primary storage?

12. ______________________

13. What was the first higher level language to receive widespread acceptance?

13. ______________________

14. What was the first higher level language used for business programming?

14. ______________________

15. What is the nonmetallic substance used in an integrated circuit?

15. ______________________

16. What computer development generated the Nobel prize for its inventors? 16. ____________

17. Who founded Apple Computer? 17.a. ____________

b. ____________

18. What is the general-purpose processor-on-a-chip of the fourth generation? 18. ____________

19. What was the first personal computer called? 19. ____________

20. Who invented the first personal computer? 20. ____________

Test Answers

Multiple Choice

1. c	6. d	11. c	16. a
2. a	7. a	12. c	17. b
3. a	8. c	13. b	18. d
4. d	9. b	14. c	19. d
5. c	10. b	15. d	20. a

True/False

1. T	6. F	11. T	16. F
2. T	7. T	12. T	17. T
3. F	8. T	13. T	18. T
4. F	9. F	14. F	19. T
5. F	10. F	15. T	20. F

Matching

1.	b	6.	e
2.	i	7.	h
3.	j	8.	d
4.	g	9.	f
5.	a	10.	c

Fill-In

1.a. input
 b. processor
 c. control unit
 d. storage
 e. output

2. transistor

3.a. The Countess of Lovelace

 b. Charles Babbage

4. Thomas J. Watson, Sr.

5. Hollerith's tabulating machine

6.a. John Atanasoff
 b. Clifford Berry
 c. the ABC

7.a. Howard Aiken
 b. the Harvard Mark I

8.a. ENIAC
 b. 1946

9. UNIVAC I

10.a. vacuum tube
 b. transistor
 c. integrated circuit
 d. microprocessor

11. magnetic core

12. magnetic tape

13. FORTRAN

14. COBOL

15. silicon

16. transistor

17.a. Steve Jobs
 b. Steve Wozniak

18. the microprocessor

19. MITS Altair

20. Ed Roberts

Close to Home

Pause for a few minutes to take a trip back through the last couple decades. Where do you fit in? How do your own personal life events - birth, graduations, and so forth - coincide with the ongoing march of the Computer Revolution?

Now let us take that a step further. Where will you fit on the continuation of the table - the history of events yet to be recorded? Some people enjoy making predictions for their own futures or, perhaps, setting some specific goals. Envision how the use of computers will affect you in the immediate future - say, the next five or ten years - then try to plan generally how you will make use of this tool in your work, in your interactions with society, and in your home.